PROGRESSIVE

Beginner RECORDER

by
Peter Gelling

Visit our Website
www.learntoplaymusic.com

The Progressive Series of Music Instruction Books, CDs, and DVDs

Acknowledgements
Cover Photograph: Phil Martin
Photographs: Phil Martin

Instruments supplied by
Silver Keys and Strings

LTP Publishing
email: info@learntoplaymusic.com
or visit our website;
www.learntoplaymusic.com

I.S.B.N. 1 864691 28 X
Order Codes: 69128

COPYRIGHT CONDITIONS
No part of this book can be reproduced in any form without written consent of the publisher. © 2001 L.T.P. Publishing Pty Ltd

CONTENTS

Introduction	Page 4
Approach to Practice	4
Using the CD	4

LESSON 1 .... Page 5
Holding the Recorder 5
How to Read the Fingering Diagram 5
The Note B 5
How to Sound a Note 6
Tonguing 6
Tuning the Recorder 6
How to Read Music 7
The Four Four Time Signature 8

LESSON 2 .... Page 9
The Half Note 9
Breath Marks 9
The Half Rest 10
The Quarter Note 10

LESSON 3 .... Page 11
The Note A 11
The Quarter Rest 11
The Note G 12
Merrily We Roll Along 12
In the Light of the Moon 13

LESSON 4 .... Page 14
The Note C 14
The Three Four Time Signature 15
The Dotted Half Note 15

LESSON 5 .... Page 16
The Note D 16
Ode to Joy 17
Aura Lee 17
Beautiful Brown Eyes 17

LESSON 6 .... Page 18
The Slur 18
Staccato 18
Austrian Waltz 19
The Whole Note 20
The Lead-in 20
When the Saints go Marchin' in 20

LESSON 7 .... Page 21
The Note F 21
In the Light of the Moon 21
Breathing Technique 22

LESSON 8 .... Page 24
The Eighth Note 24
Shortnin' Bread 24
Sharp Signs, The Note F Sharp 25
Key Signatures 26
The Galway Piper 26
The Tie 26
Mary Ann 26

LESSON 9 .... Page 27
The Note E 27
The Volga Boatman 27
The Common Time Signature 28
Gypsy Dance 28

LESSON 10 .... Page 29
The Note Low D 29
The Octave 30
We Wish You a Merry Christmas 30
Shortnin' Bread 31
Goodnight Irene 31

LESSON 11 .... Page 32
The Note Low C 32
The C Major Scale 32
The Key of C Major 33
Lavender's Blue 33
Botany Bay 34

LESSON 12 .... Page 35
The Dotted Quarter Note 35
Morning Has Broken 35
First and Second Endings 36
Jingle Bells 36
Mussi Den 36
Syncopation 37
Swing Low Sweet Chariot 37
Tom Dooley 38
The Sloop John B 38

LESSON 13 .... Page 39
Flat Signs, The Note B Flat 39
Flat Key Signatures 40
All Through the Night 40
Oh Susanna 40
God Rest Ye Merry Gentlemen 41
In Olden Days 41

LESSON 14 .... Page 42
The Note High E 42
My Bonnie Lies Over the Ocean 43

LESSON 15 .... Page 44
12 Bar Blues 44
Playing Riffs 44
The Eighth Rest 45
The Natural Sign 45
Creepy Blues 46

LESSON 16 .... Page 47
The Triplet 47
Triplet Blues 47
Swing Rhythms 48
Riffin' the Blues 49
St James Infirmary 49
Battle Hymn of the Republic 50
Swing That Thing 50

Recorder Fingerings Index 51

INTRODUCTION

Progressive Beginner Recorder will show you all the basics of recorder playing and reading music. The book is suitable for anyone who wants to learn to play the recorder. No previous musical knowledge or experience is necessary. The book covers all the natural notes on the recorder from middle C up to the E a tenth above middle C, along with one sharp and one flat. All essential articulations such as basic tonguing, slurring and staccato playing are also covered. Music essentials such as time signatures, key signatures, note and rest values, repeats and first and second endings are also covered. Each new note and technique is introduced separately and all examples sound great and are fun to play. The book also features a chart listing all fingerings for the recorder. On completion of the book, you will already be able to play many tunes and be making great sounds. You will also be ready to begin playing with other musicians and to move on to more advanced study of the recorder or to begin playing a larger wind instrument such as saxophone or clarinet. In the early stages of playing any musical instrument, it is helpful to have the guidance of an experienced teacher. This will also help you keep to a schedule and obtain weekly goals.

DVD's AND VIDEOS AVAILABLE

There is a **DVD** (or VHS video) available to accompany this book, demonstrating all the examples with live footage and easy to follow diagrams. There are also DVD's available for most of the other titles in the *Progressive Beginner* series. For more information, contact:

LTP Publishing
email: info@learntoplaymusic.com
or visit our website;
www.learntoplaymusic.com

APPROACH TO PRACTICE

It is important to have a correct approach to practice. You will benefit more from several short practices (e.g. 15-30 minutes per day) than one or two long sessions per week. This is especially so in the early stages, because of the basic nature of the material being studied and also because your lips and facial muscles are still developing. In a practice session you should divide your time evenly between the study of new material and the revision of past work. It is a common mistake for semi-advanced students to practice only the pieces they can already play well. Although this is more enjoyable, it is not a very satisfactory method of practice. You should also try to correct mistakes and experiment with new ideas.

USING THE COMPACT DISC

It is recommended that you have a copy of the accompanying compact disc that includes all the examples in this book. The book shows you where to put your fingers and what technique to use and the recording lets you hear how each example should sound. Practice the examples slowly at first, gradually increasing the tempo. Once you are confident you can play the example, playing evenly without stopping the beat, try playing along with the recording. You will hear a drum beat at the beginning of each example, to lead you into the example and to help you keep time. To play along with the CD your recorder must be in tune with it. To learn how to tune your recorder to the CD see page 6. A small diagram of a compact disc with a number as shown below indicates a recorded example. The first track on the CD is the **B** note used for tuning on page 6.

1 B note — CD Track Number

LESSON ONE

HOLDING THE RECORDER

The numbers on the fingers show which fingers should be used to press down the keys as shown in the fingering diagrams at the bottom of the page.

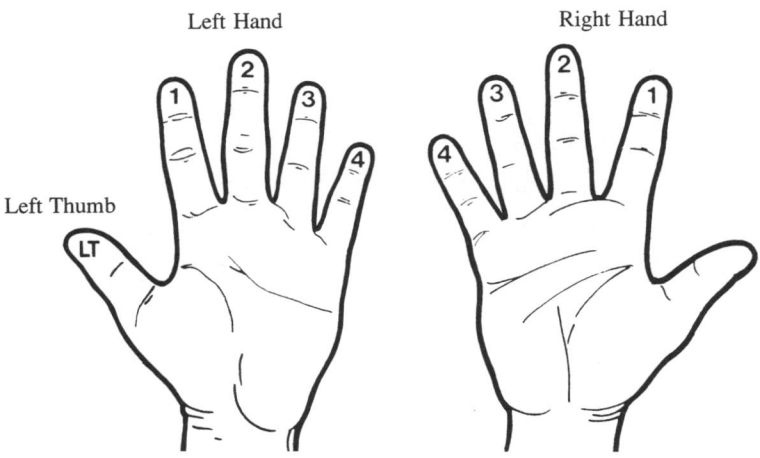

HOW TO HOLD THE RECORDER

To learn how to hold the recorder, it is best to place your hands in position to play the note **B**. The first step is to cover the hole at the back of the recorder with your left thumb and cover the top hole on the front of the recorder with the first finger of your left hand. In this position, you have the fingering for the note **B** as shown in the diagram below. Next place your right thumb on the back of the recorder lower down the body. The main role of the right thumb is to support the weight of the recorder as you play.

THE NOTE B

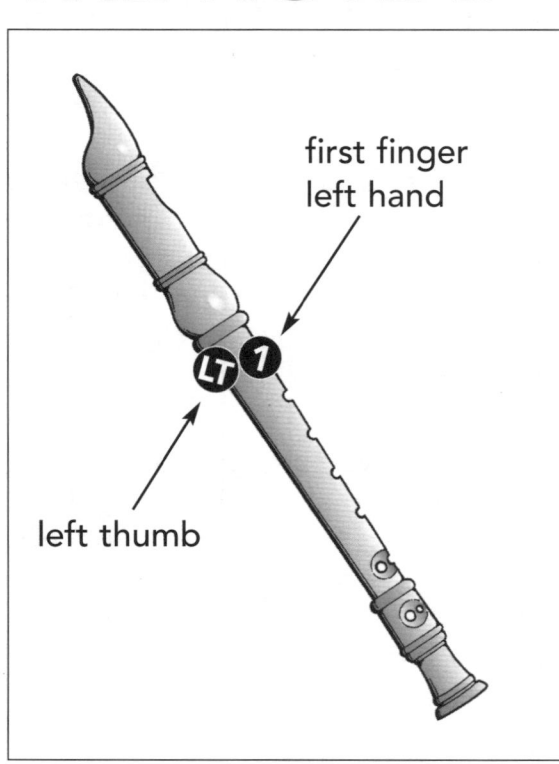

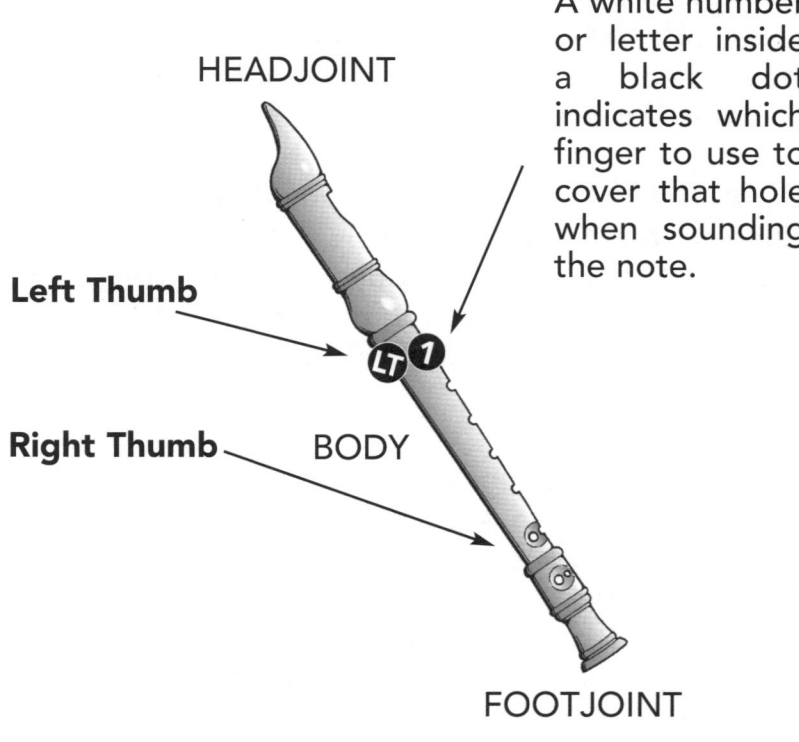

A white number or letter inside a black dot indicates which finger to use to cover that hole when sounding the note.

HOW TO SOUND A NOTE

The first note you will learn to play is the **B** note shown on the previous page. Place your fingers in position to play the note and put the tip of the recorder into your mouth. Use your lips to seal off any air from escaping out the sides of your mouth and blow smoothly and steadily into the recorder. Don't blow too hard or start the note too suddenly, or you may cause the note to sound at the wrong pitch or cause the recorder to squeak. If you are unsure what the note should sound like, listen to example 2 on the CD and try to imitate it.

TONGUING

To control the beginning and end of a note, the technique of **tonguing** is used. To prepare for this technique whisper the sound **'taa'**. The sound begins with your tongue sitting behind your top teeth, blocking the passage of air, and you make the **'taa'** sound by quickly withdrawing it, and letting a stream of air begin from your outgoing breath.

The next step is to do this with the recorder in position to play a **B** note, with your tongue lightly on the hole in the mouthpiece. As you withdraw your tongue, the note will have a well articulated beginning. The "**t**" part of the sound gives the note a definite starting point, and the "**aa**" part of the sound keeps your throat open so that the flow of air remains constant and the note sounds even. To end the note, you put your tongue back on the reed rather than stopping your breath. This will end the note as crisply as it started. It is worth practicing the tonguing technique many times on a single note until you are comfortable with it.

TUNING YOUR RECORDER TO THE CD

The pitch of the recorder can be altered by either pushing the headjoint further onto the body or pulling it back a bit. Before you begin tuning to the CD, make sure the headjoint is not pushed fully onto the body, or you may have no room to move if your recorder is out of tune.

The first track on the CD contains a **B** note for you to tune to. Cue it to the start of the first track and then play a **B** note. Listen carefully to the sound and try to keep it in your mind when you finish playing the note. Then start the CD and see if the B note sounds the same as the one you just played. If it does, you are already in tune with the recording.

If you think your B note is lower than the B note on the CD, you can make it higher by pushing the headjoint gently a little further onto the body. Be careful to move the headjoint only a small amount at a time, or you may put the instrument out of tune in the opposite direction; i.e. you may make the note sound too sharp instead of too flat. Once you have moved the mouthpiece, play the note again and check it against the CD. Repeat this process until your B note and the CD note sound the same.

If your B note is higher than the recording, you will have to move the headjoint in the opposite direction – pulling it back out away from the body a small amount and then checking your note against the CD. Once again, repeat the process if necessary until your B note and the CD note sound the same.

If you have trouble hearing the differences in pitch and matching them evenly, don't worry, this is common and tuning will become easier as your lips and facial muscles develop and you get a better sense of the sounds of notes in general.

HOW TO READ MUSIC

These five lines are called the **staff** or **stave**.

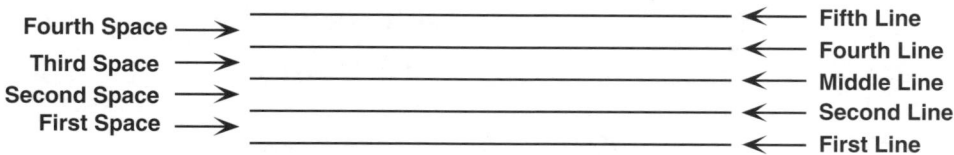

THE TREBLE CLEF

 This symbol is called a **treble clef**. There is a treble clef at the beginning of every line of recorder music.

THE TREBLE STAFF

A staff with a treble clef written on it is called a **treble staff**.

MUSIC NOTES

There are only seven letters used for notes in music. They are:
A B C D E F G

These notes are known as the **musical alphabet.**
Recorder music notes are written in the spaces and on the lines of the treble staff.

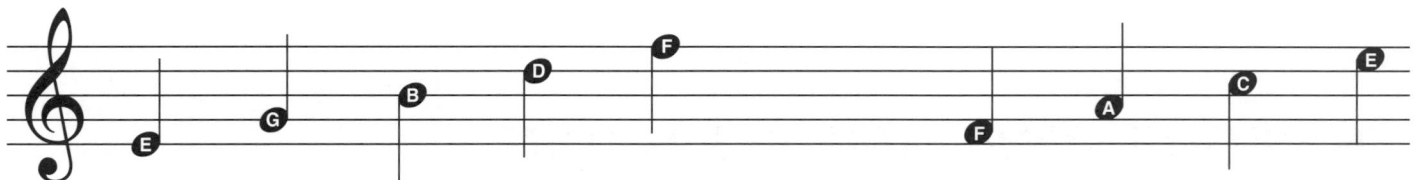

To remember the notes on the lines of the treble staff, say:
Every **G**ood **B**oy **D**eserves **F**ruit.

The notes in the spaces of the treble staff spell:
F A C E

THE QUARTER NOTE

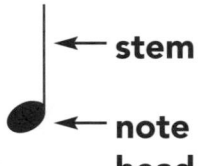
← stem
← note head

This music note is called a **quarter note**.
A quarter note lasts for **one beat**.

NOTE AND REST VALUES

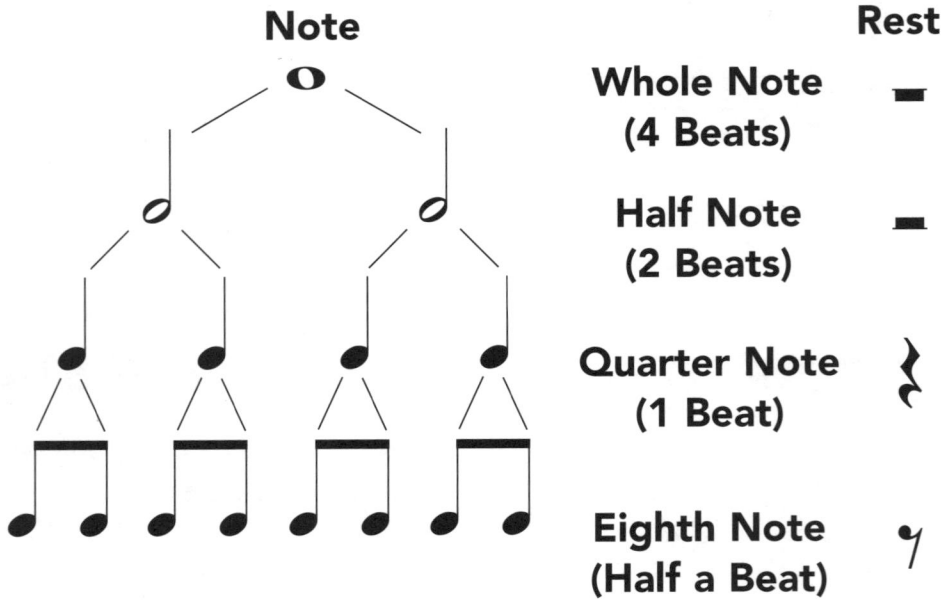

Bar lines are drawn across the staff, which divides the music into sections called **Bars** or **Measures**. A **Double bar line** signifies either the end of the music, or the end of an important section of it.

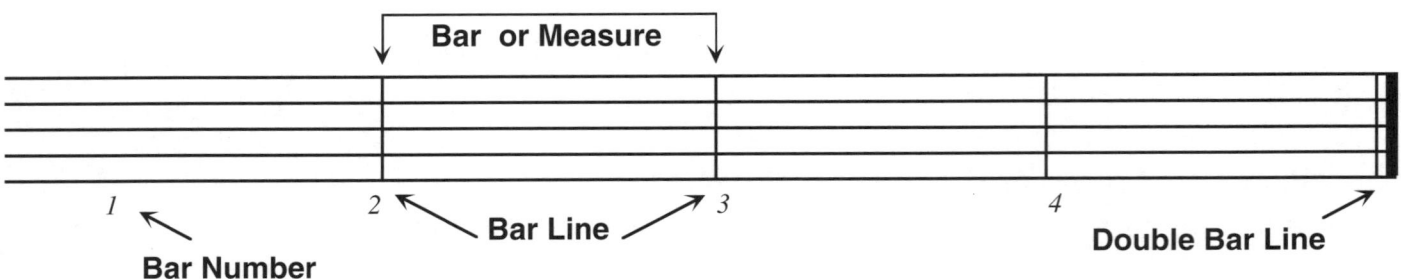

THE FOUR FOUR TIME SIGNATURE

These two numbers are called the **four four time signature**.
They are placed after the treble clef. The $\frac{4}{4}$ time signature tells you there are four beats in each bar. There are **four** quarter notes in one bar of music in $\frac{4}{4}$ time.

LESSON TWO

THE HALF NOTE

This music note is called a **half note**. It has a value of **two** beats. There are **two** half notes in one bar of 4/4 time.

Count: 1 2

THE NOTE B

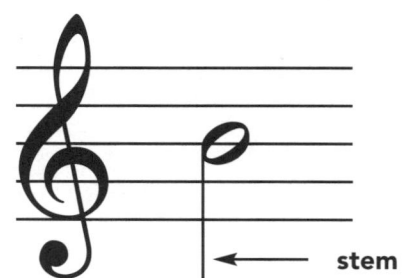

The note **B** is written on the **middle** line of the staff.

CHORD SYMBOLS

If you look at example 2 at the bottom of the page, you will notice two lines of letters and symbols above the staff (**Em**, **B7** etc.) These are **chord symbols** which indicate the harmony to be played by accompanying instruments such as keyboard or guitar.

KEEPING TIME

Before you play example 2, count **1 2 3 4 1 2 3 4** several times to get a feel for the rhythm. As you play the example, count mentally as you play and tap your foot to help you keep time. Count **1 2** for the first half note in each bar and **3 4** for the second half note. To be sure you develop a good sense of time right from the beginning, it is recommended that you **always practice with a metronome or drum machine**. Each example on the CD begins with four drum beats. Count along with these beats to help you establish the right tempo (speed) for each example.

BREATH MARKS (▼)

Take a quick, deep breath from your diaphragm every time you see this mark ▼. Be careful not to lose your timing when you breathe. Counting as you play should help you become more confident with this. Breathing technique is discussed in detail on pages 21 and 22.

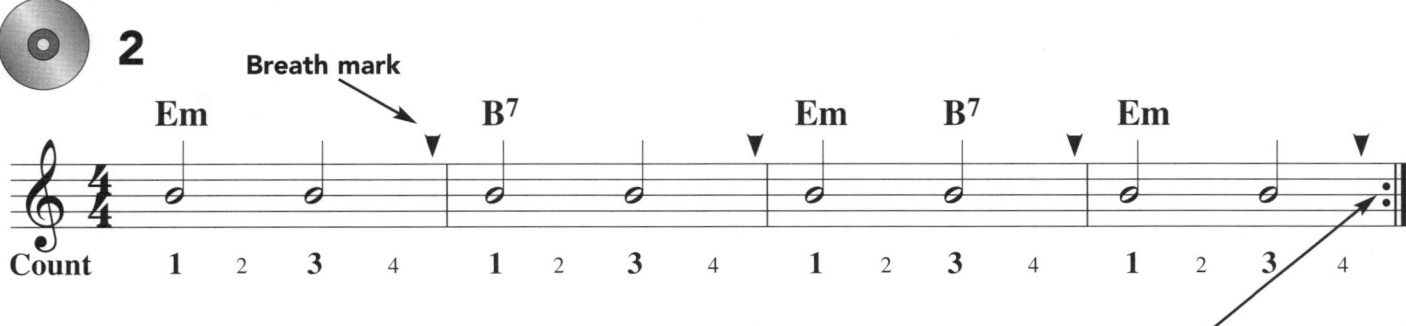

The **big** numbers **1** and **3** tell you to play the note. The **small** numbers 2 and 4 tell you to sustain it until the next note. Notice that there are four beats in each bar.

These two dots are called a **repeat sign**. This means that you play the exercise again from the start.

THE HALF REST

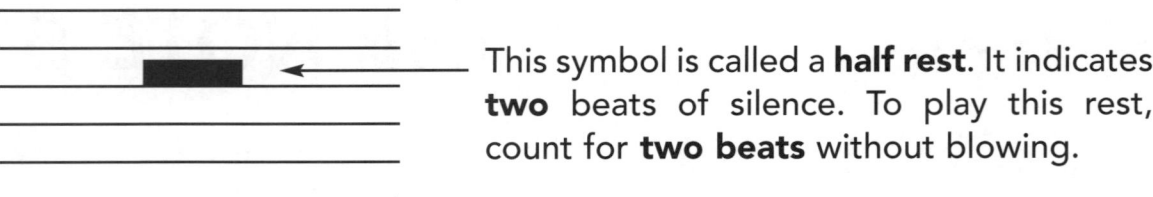

This symbol is called a **half rest**. It indicates **two** beats of silence. To play this rest, count for **two beats** without blowing.

Count: 1   2

Small counting numbers are used under rests.

 3

This example uses half notes along with half rests. Anywhere a rest appears in a piece of music is usually the best place to take a breath. To get into the habit of breathing when you see a rest, breathe on each of the rests shown here, even if you don't need a breath.

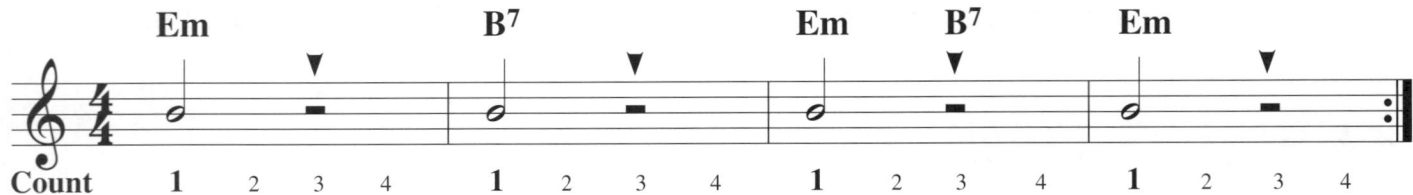

THE QUARTER NOTE

 This music note is called a **quarter note**. It lasts for **one** beat. There are four quarter notes in one bar of 4/4 time.

Count: 1

 4

This example contains both quarter notes and half notes. Make sure you tongue each note.

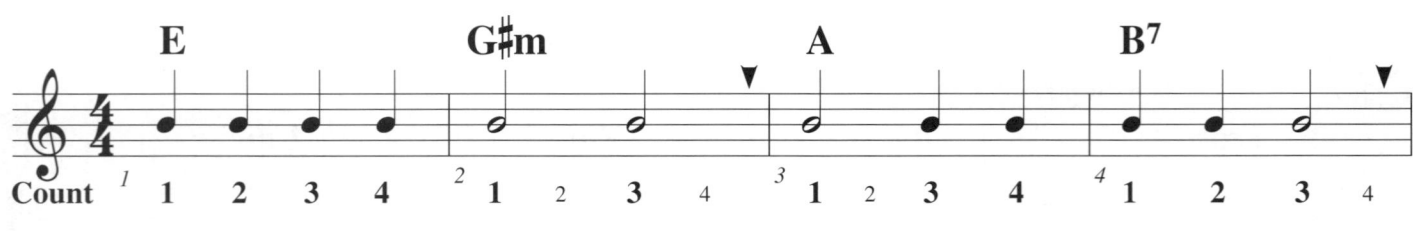

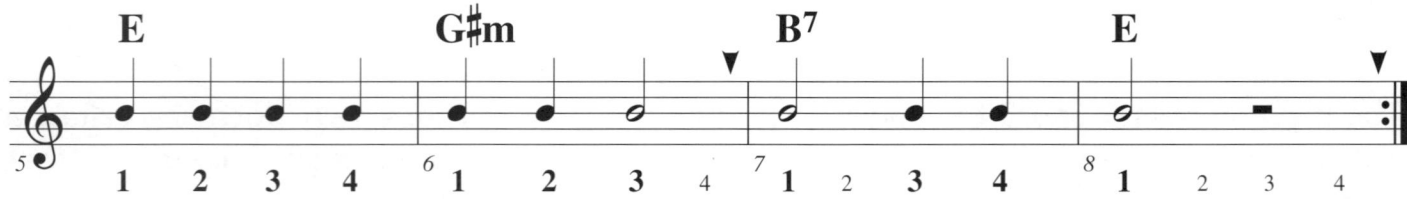

LESSON THREE

THE NOTE A

A Note

The note **A** is written in the **second** space of the staff.

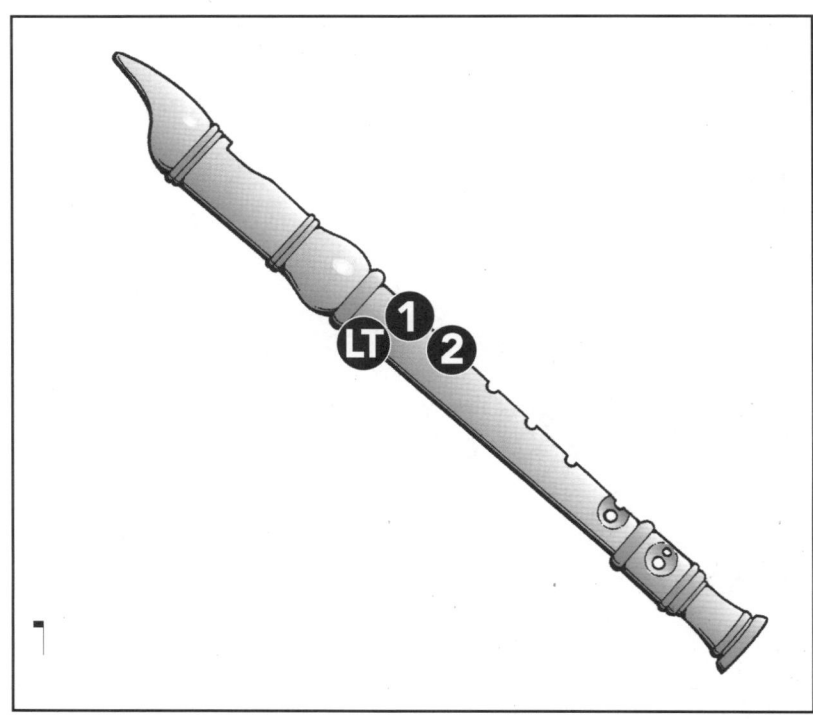

 **5**

The following example combines the note **A** with the note **B**. Listen carefully to the notes as you play them and try to produce a **strong, even tone**. Pay attention to the breath marks and get in the habit of breathing each time you see one.

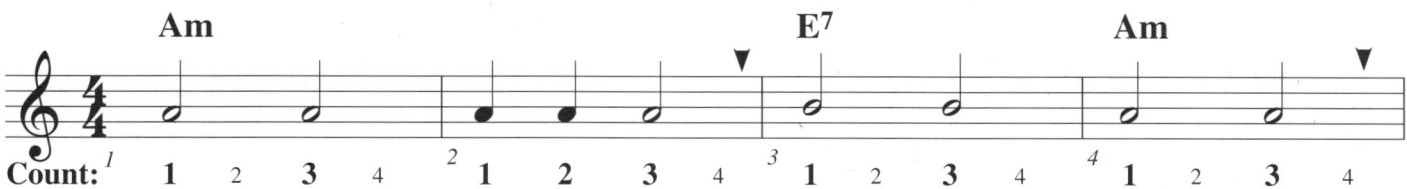

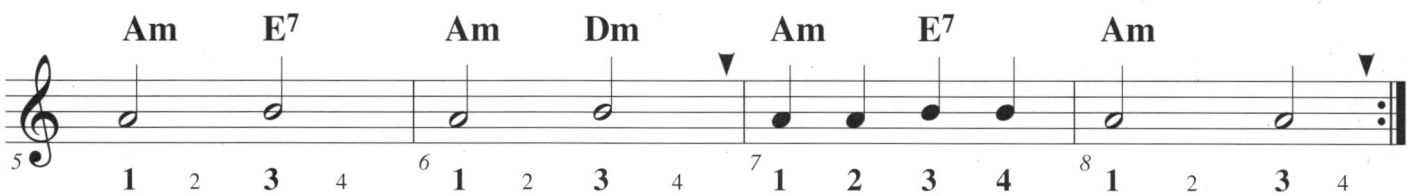

THE QUARTER REST

This symbol is a **quarter rest.** It indicates **one beat of silence**. Do not play any note. Remember that small counting numbers are placed under rests.

Count: 1

 **6**

This example makes frequent use of the quarter rest and once again moves between the notes **B** and **A**. Be sure to count mentally as you play. There are no breath marks written above the notes in this example. You are free to breathe anywhere a rest appears.

THE NOTE G

G Note

This note is a **G** note. It is written on the **second** line of the staff.

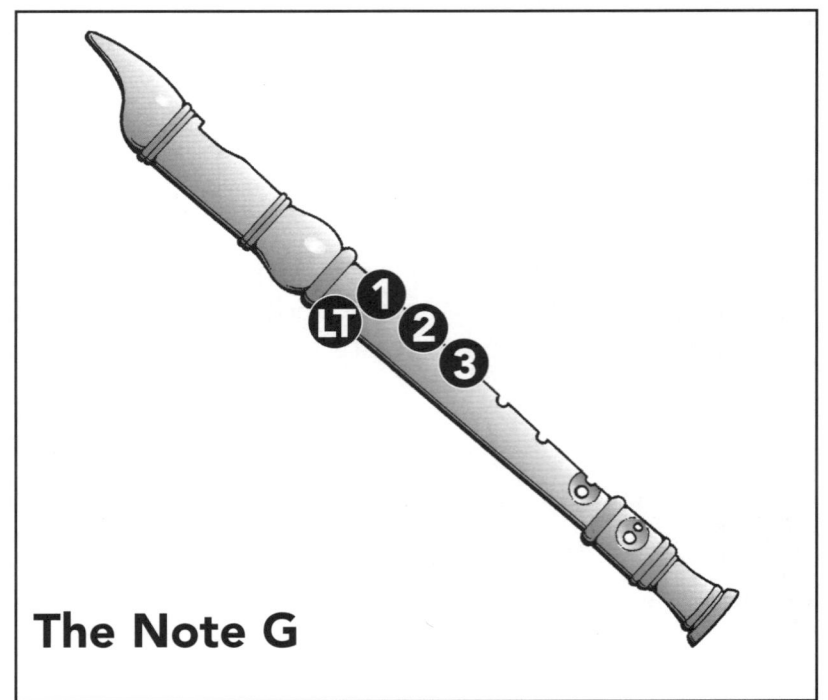

The Note G

 **7 Merrily We Roll Along**

This traditional children's song uses the note **G** along with the other two notes you have learnt.

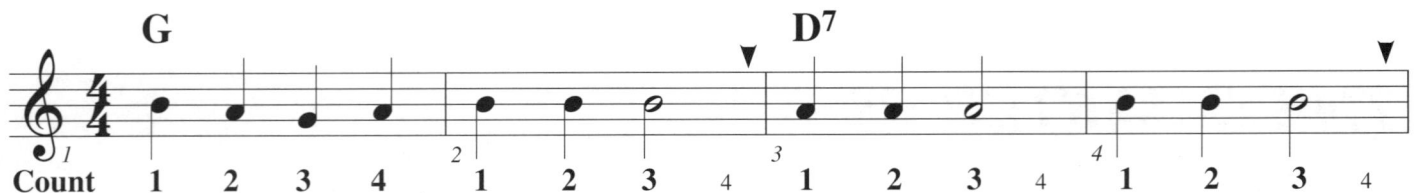

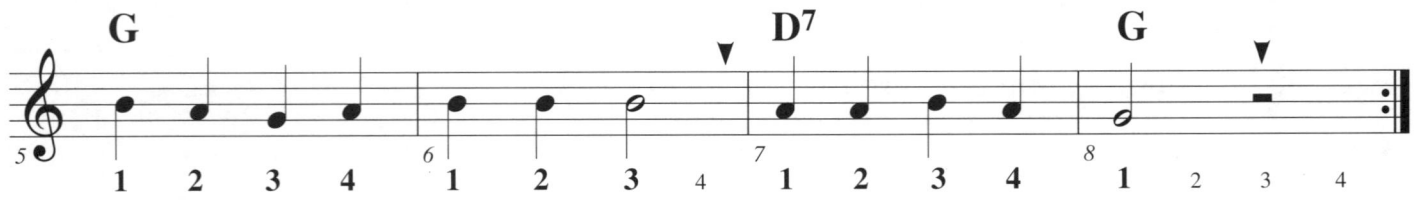

Here are three more tunes which make use of the notes **B**, **A** and **G**.

 **8**   **In the Light of the Moon**

 **9**

Notes written below the middle line of a staff usually have their stems going **up**. The stem for the note **B** can go **up or down.** Notice the two possible directions for the stems of the note **B** in this example. The stem direction makes no difference to the way the note is played.

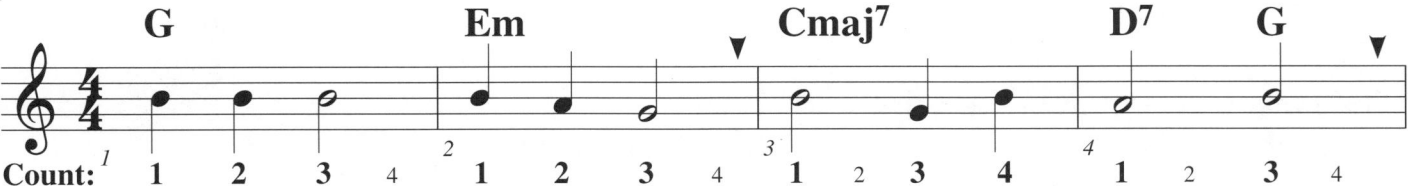

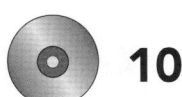 **10**

Once again there are no breath marks written here. Breathe anywhere a rest appears and be sure to take a good breath in bar 8, as there are no more rests until bar 12.

LESSON FOUR

THE NOTE C

Notes written **above** the middle line of a staff usually have their stems going **down.**

C Note

← stem

The note **C** is written in the **third** space of the staff.

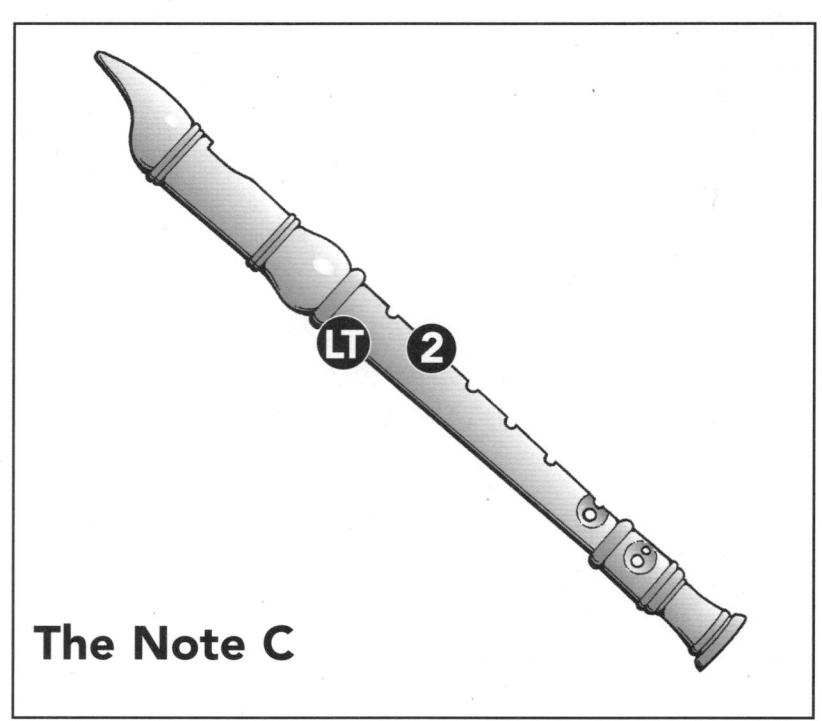

The Note C

Once you have memorized the fingering for the note **C**, play examples 11 and 12 which combine this new note with the other notes you have learnt.

 **11**

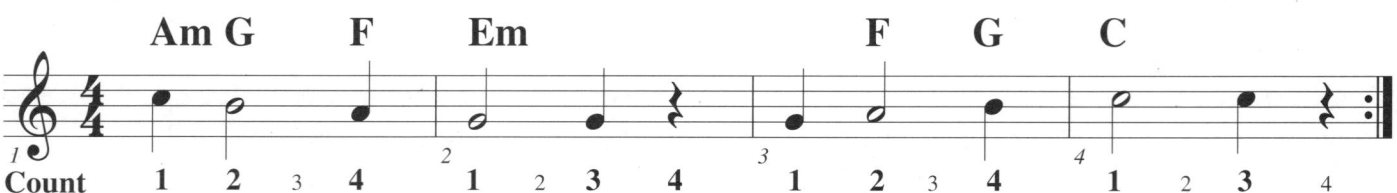

 **12**

THE THREE FOUR TIME SIGNATURE

This time signature is called the **three four** time signature. It tells you there are **three** beats in each bar. Three four time is also known as waltz time. There are **three** quarter notes in one bar of 3/4 time.

 **13**

THE DOTTED HALF NOTE

A **dot** written after a note extends its value by **half**.
A dot after a half note means that you hold it for **three** beats.
One dotted half note makes one bar of music in 3/4 time.

 **14**

Here is a typical example of the way dotted half notes are used in 3/4 time. As there are no rests in this example, breath marks are placed in every fourth bar after a dotted half note. From this point on breath marks will only be placed every four bars in most examples to encourage you to develop more breath control. However, you can still breathe more often if you need to.

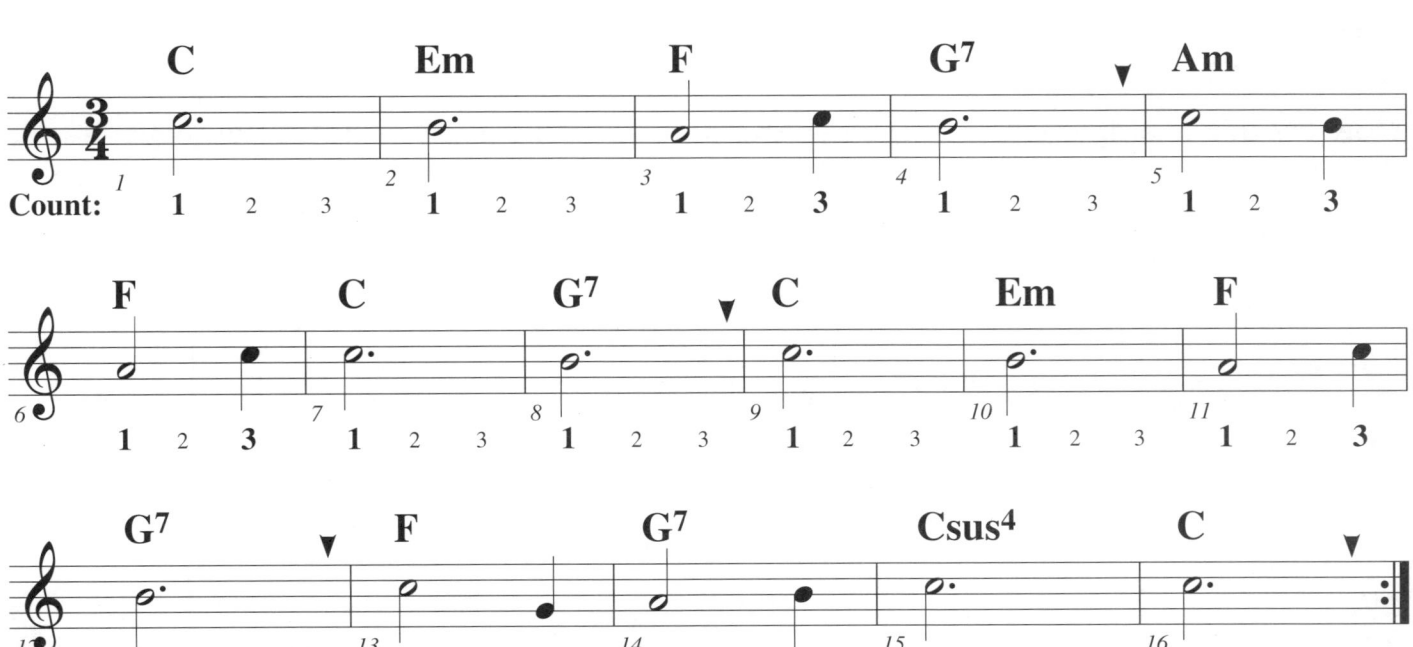

LESSON FIVE

THE NOTE D

D Note

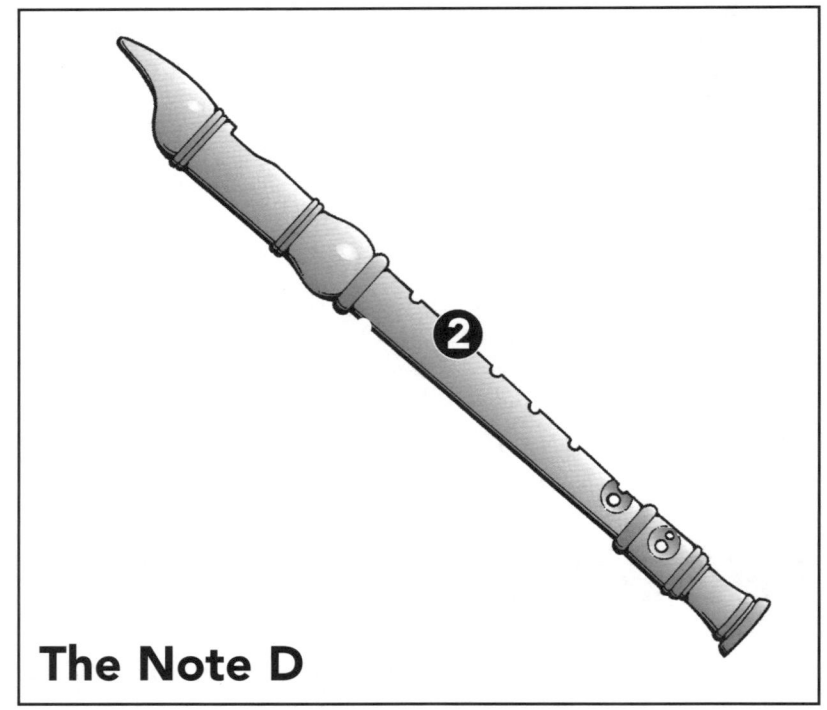

The Note D

The note **D** is written on the **fourth** line of the staff.

The following example alternates between the notes **D** and **C**. The only difference in fingering here is that the thumb is not used for the **D** note.

 **15**

 **16**

Now try this example which combines the note **D** with the other notes you have learnt. Breath marks are only shown every four bars here, but breathe every two bars if necessary. As your playing develops you won't need to breathe as often as in the beginning stages.

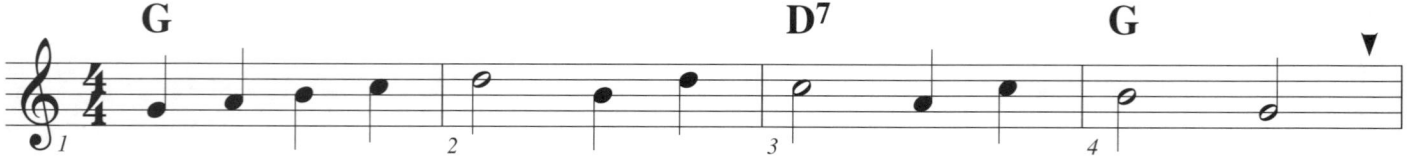

Because you have to think about moving your thumb as well as the other fingers, it may take some time to become comfortable changing between **D** and all the other notes. Here are some more songs to give you extra practice at moving between all the notes you have learnt.

 ## 17   Ode to Joy
Beethoven

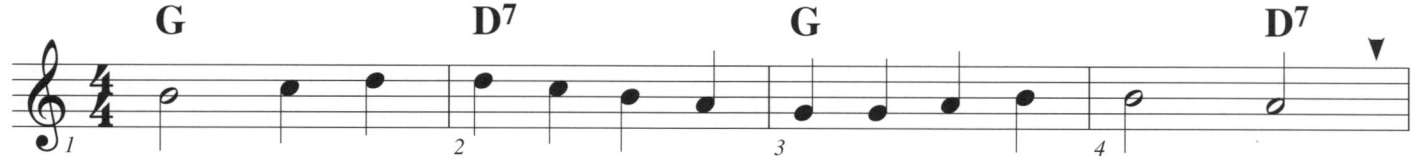

 ## 18   Aura Lee

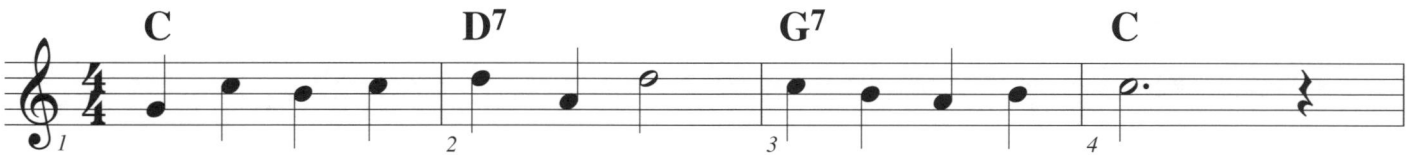

 ## 19   Beautiful Brown Eyes

This one is in ¾ time. There are no breath marks written here and no rests until the final bar, which means you will have to find your own places to breathe. A good place to breathe is at the end of any of the dotted half notes, just before you play the following note.

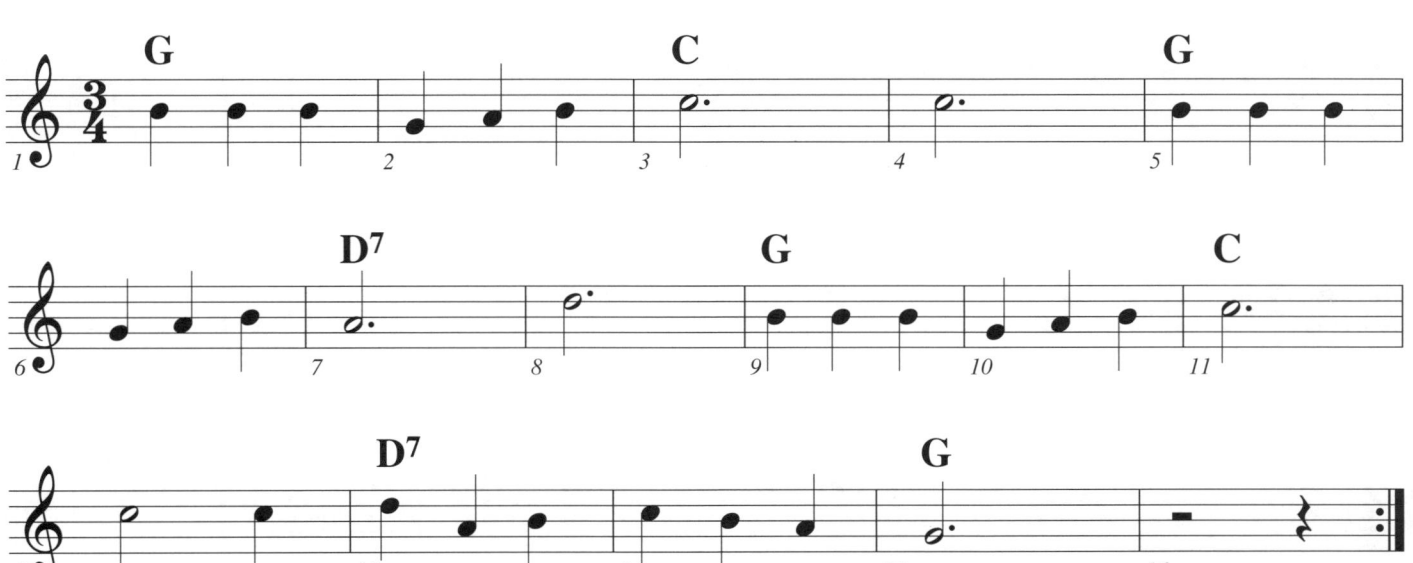

LESSON SIX

THE SLUR

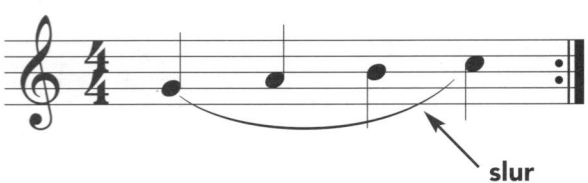

Tongue only the **first** note.

A **slur** is a curved line above or below two or more different notes. It tells you to play the notes smoothly. Playing smoothly is called **legato.** To play legato, only tongue the **first** note of the group and keep blowing while you change your finger positions for the other notes.

Here are some more examples to help you become more familiar with slurs. Remember to tongue only the first note of each group of notes connected by the slur.

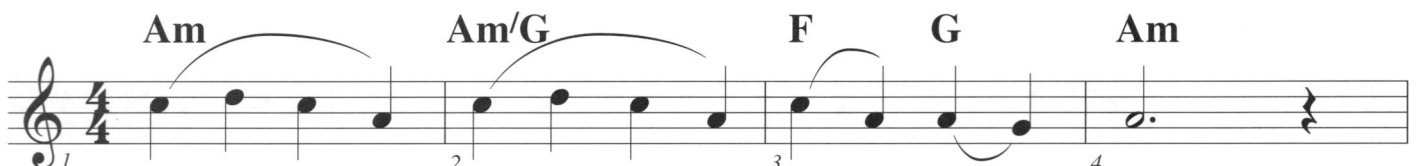

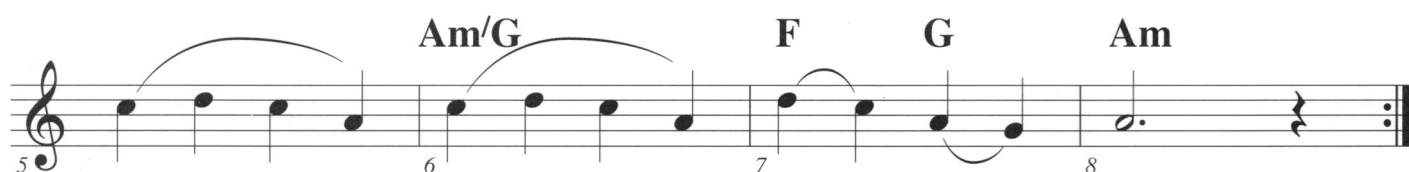

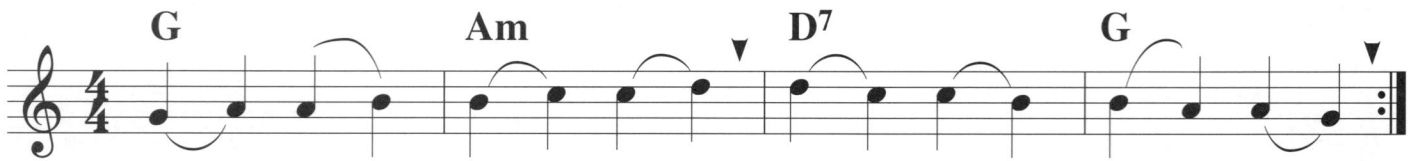

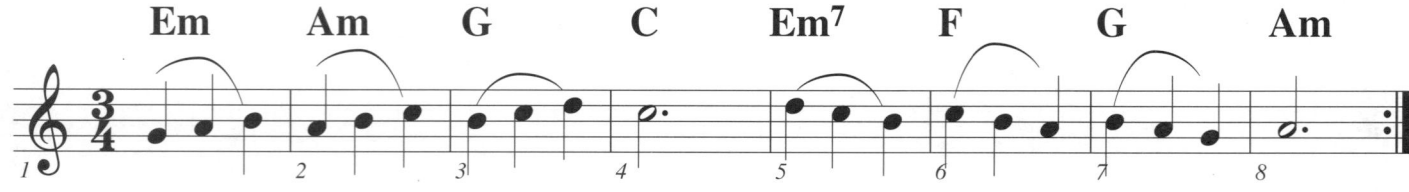

STACCATO

A dot above or below a note tells you to play the note **staccato.** Staccato means to play a note short and separate from other notes. This is the opposite of legato. To play a note staccato, make a short '**t**' action with your tongue, and cut off your breath as soon as you tongue the note.

To gain more control of the way you play notes, it is a good idea to practice alternating between ordinary tonguing and staccato tonguing as shown in this example.

COMBINING DIFFERENT ARTICULATIONS

 **Austrian Waltz**

This song contains both staccato and slur marks. This means there are three different techniques used to play the various notes, i.e. ordinary tonguing, slurring, and staccato tonguing. These different ways of playing the notes are called **articulations**. Articulations are used to create variety of expression in music.

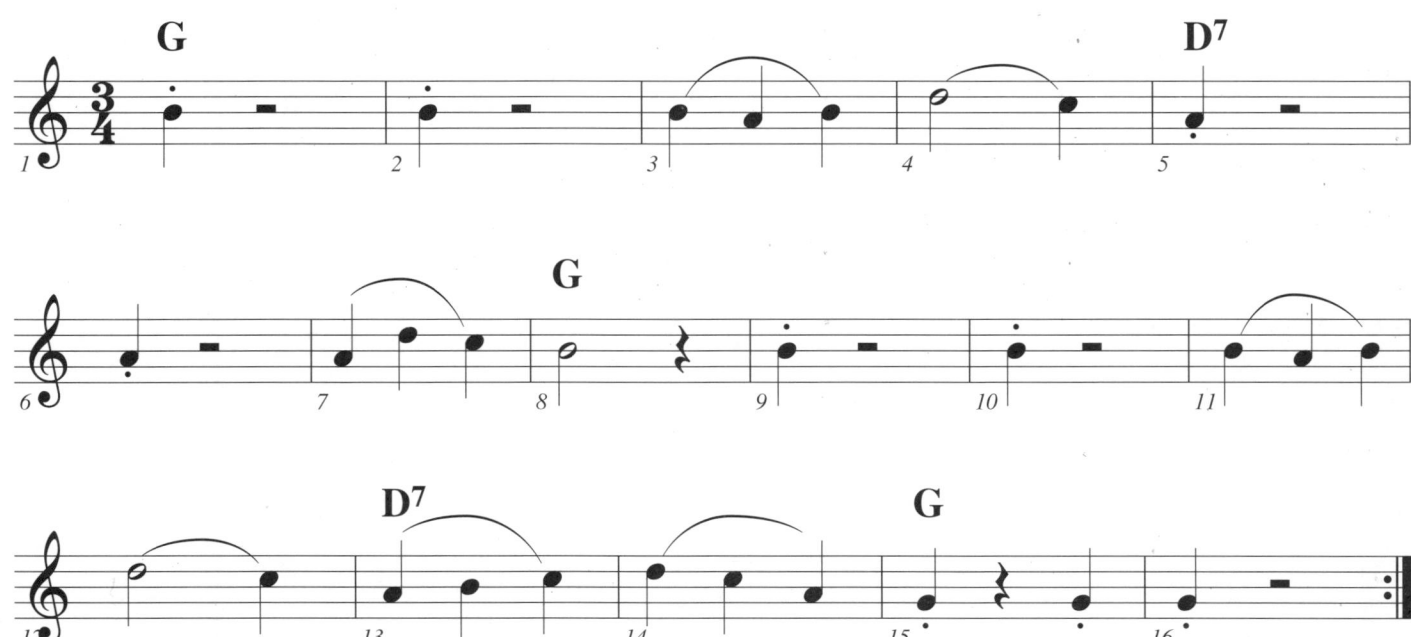

THE WHOLE NOTE

 This is a **whole note**.
It lasts for **four** beats.
Count: **1** 2 3 4   There is **one** whole note in one bar of 4/4 time.

27

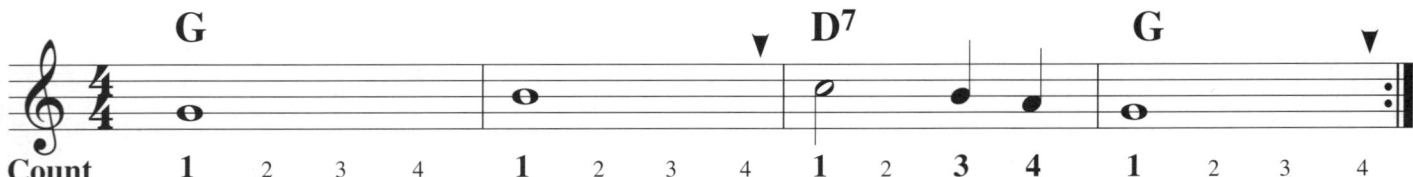

THE LEAD-IN

Sometimes a song does not begin on the first beat of a bar. Any notes which come before the first full bar are called **lead-in notes** (or pick-up notes). When lead-in notes are used, the last bar is also incomplete. The notes in the lead-in and the notes in the last bar add up to one full bar. Here is an example.

28 **When the Saints go Marchin' in**

This song is an early Jazz standard made popular by brass bands in New Orleans. It contains **three lead-in notes**. On the recording there are **five** drumbeats to introduce this song.

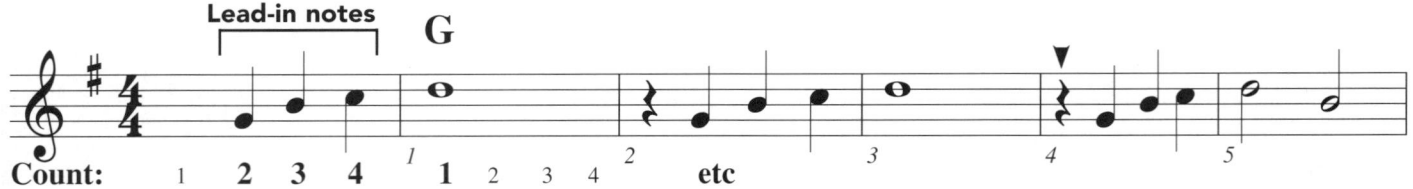

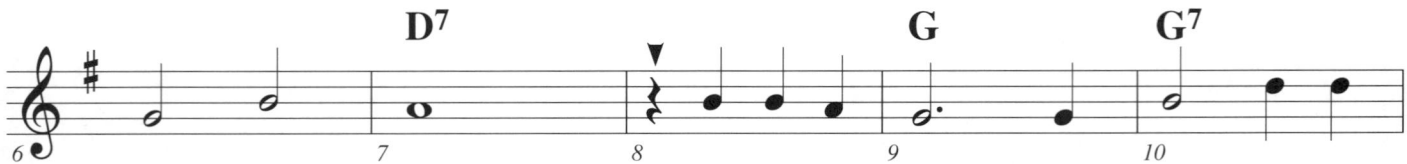

LESSON SEVEN

THE NOTE F

F Note

The note **F** is written in the **first** space of the staff.

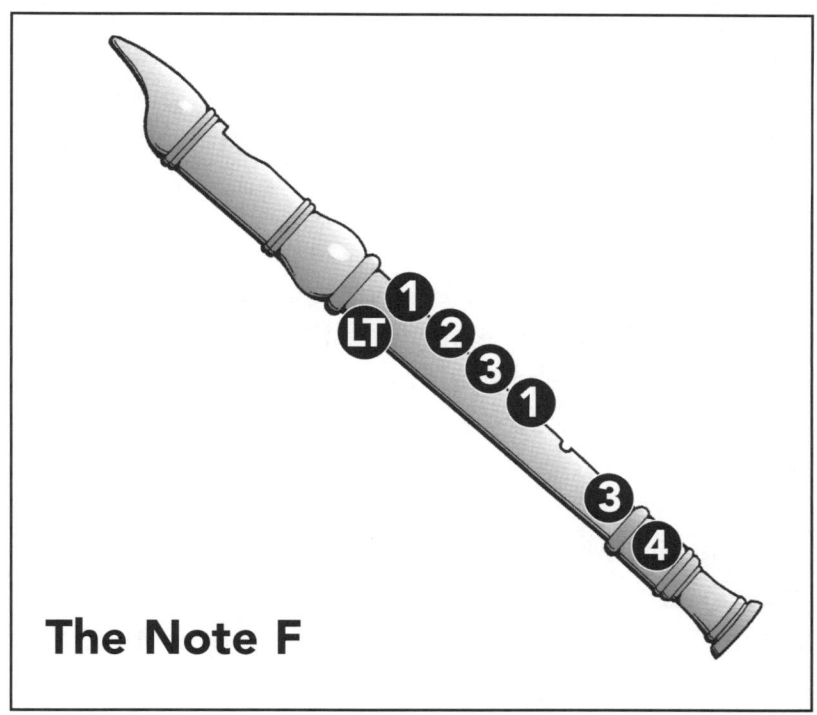

The Note F

As demonstrated in the above diagram, the note **F** requires the use of both the left and right hands. This may take some time to gain control of, so take the following examples slowly at first and be patient. Your co-ordination will improve with practice. You will notice that your third and fourth fingers on the right hand are covering double holes. It is important to cover both holes with each finger in order to get the correct sound.

 **29**

 **30   In the Light of the Moon**

Here is another version of a song you learnt in lesson 3, this time starting on the note **F**.

BREATHING TECHNIQUE

One of the most important elements of playing any wind instrument is a consistent and relaxed approach to breathing and breath control. A good player always produces a strong, even tone and sounds relaxed regardless of the difficulty of the music being played. Outlined below are some breathing exercises which will help you gain more control over the way you breathe when playing and give you a solid consistent approach which will eventually become automatic, enabling you to forget about breathing and concentrate totally on the music you are making.

A good way of developing your breathing technique is the use of visualisation. When you breathe **in**, think of an inflatable life raft which fills automatically when you pull out the plug. This will help you equate breathing in with relaxation. When you breathe **out**, think of a tube of toothpaste being slowly squeezed from the end (not the middle). This will help you use your breath economically in a controlled manner.

It is important to develop the habit of controlling your breathing from your diaphragm muscle (shown in the diagram below). As you breathe **in**, let the diaphragm relax downwards and allow the lungs to fill with air right to the bottom. Then breathe **out slowly**, squeezing gently from the diaphragm (like the tube of toothpaste) and see how long you can sustain your outgoing breath. The more control you have of your diaphrhagm, the easier you will find breathing when you play.

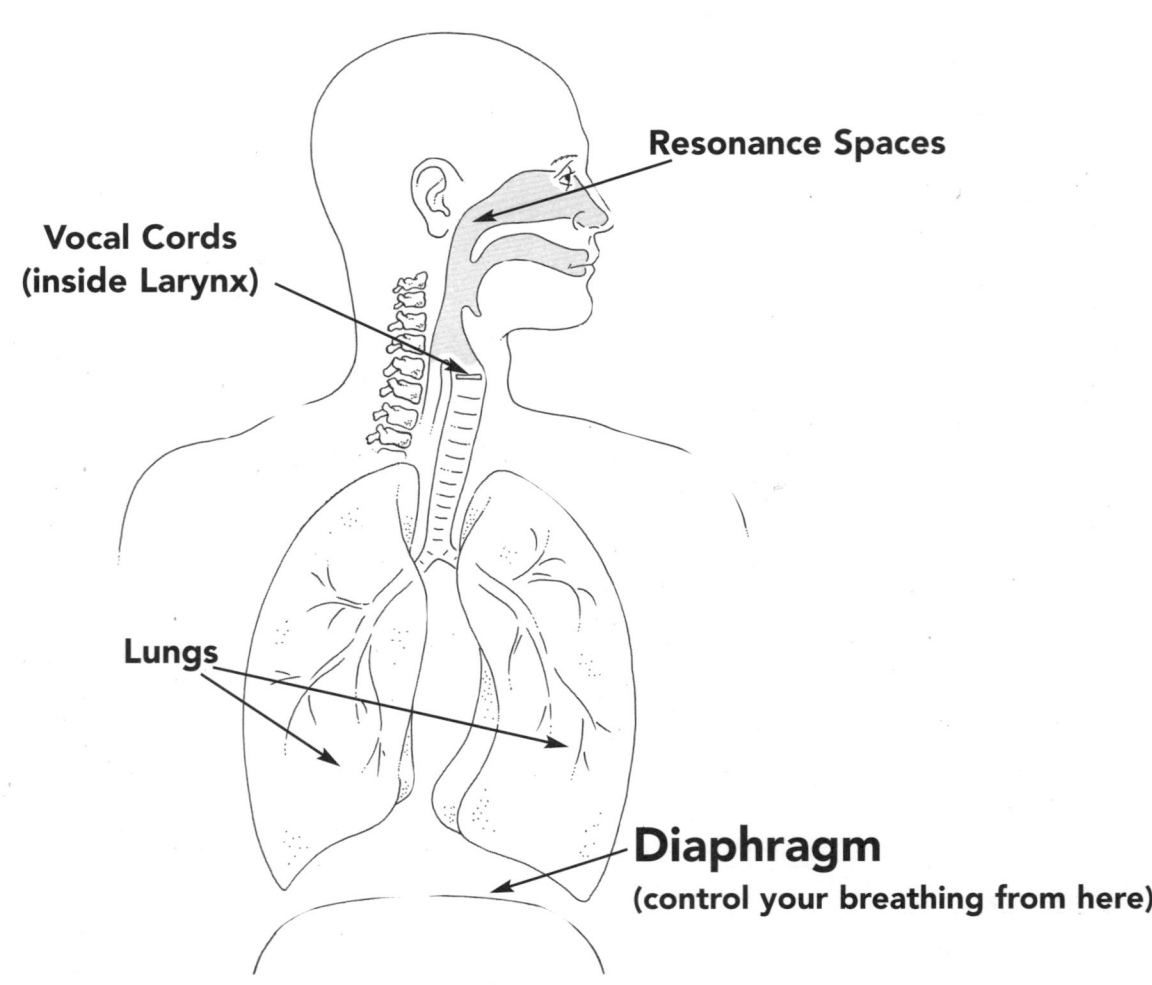

Breathing Exercise

This example makes frequent use of whole notes. Practicing long notes is an excellent way of developing your tone as well as breath control. Aim for a **strong**, **even tone** throughout the example.

OTHER USEFUL EXERCISES

When playing wind instruments, it is common to use more air, movement and muscle activity than necessary. There are two common exercises which are useful for learning to use less force and less air when playing. The first of these is to slowly blow up a balloon, using slow sustained breaths controlled from the diaphragm. The idea is to take a comfortable breath using the technique described earlier and then breathe into the balloon using an even sustained amount of air pressure. Repeat this until the balloon is full.

The second exercise is to **sing** a melody in front of a lighted candle. This requires a more subtle release of air than blowing up a balloon, as the idea is to sing with as little effect on the flame of the candle as possible. Once you can sustain a note without moving the flame much, try beginning the note softly and gradually increasing the volume, then reverse the process. You could also try singing a whole verse from a song. As with all aspects of musicianship, be patient and you will see great improvement as long as you continue to practice.

LESSON EIGHT

THE EIGHTH NOTE

🔘 31 How to Count Eighth Notes

Written	1	+	2	+	3	+	4	+
Say	1	and	2	and	3	and	4	and

🔘 32

When you begin playing songs containing eighth notes, take them slowly at first until you gain control of all the notes. Once you are comfortable with the whole tune, gradually increase the tempo until you can play along with the CD. Since there are more notes now, you may need to breathe every two bars at first. You do not have to wait for a breath mark to breathe. Most sheet music does not contain breath marks so it is up to you to decide the best place to breathe.

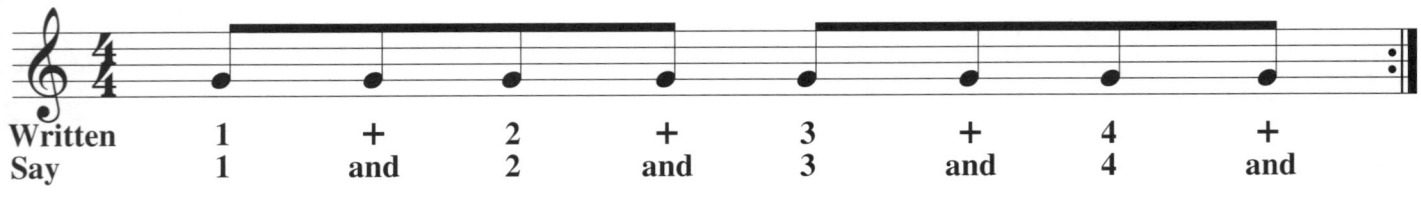

🔘 33 Shortnin' Bread

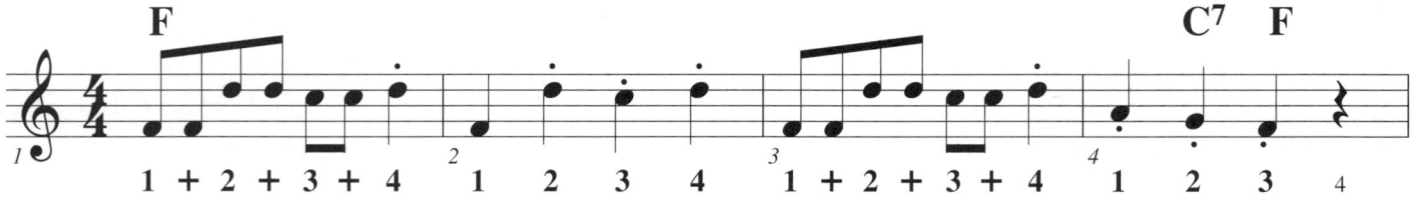

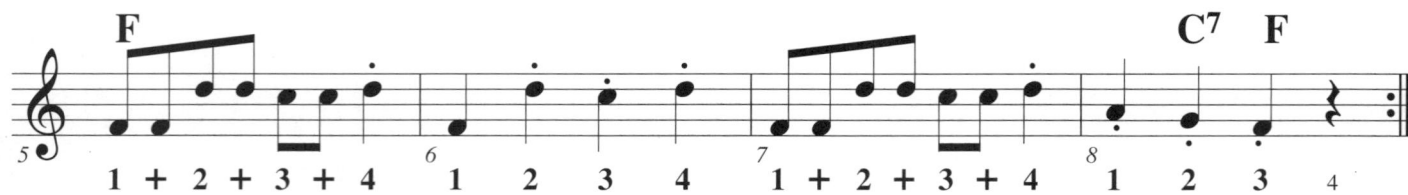

SHARP SIGNS

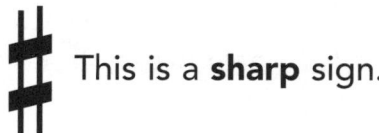 This is a **sharp** sign. When a sharp sign is placed in front of a note it raises the pitch of the note by **one semitone**. Thus the note **F#** is one semitone **higher** than F.

THE NOTE F#

F# Note

A sharp sign is always placed **before** the note.

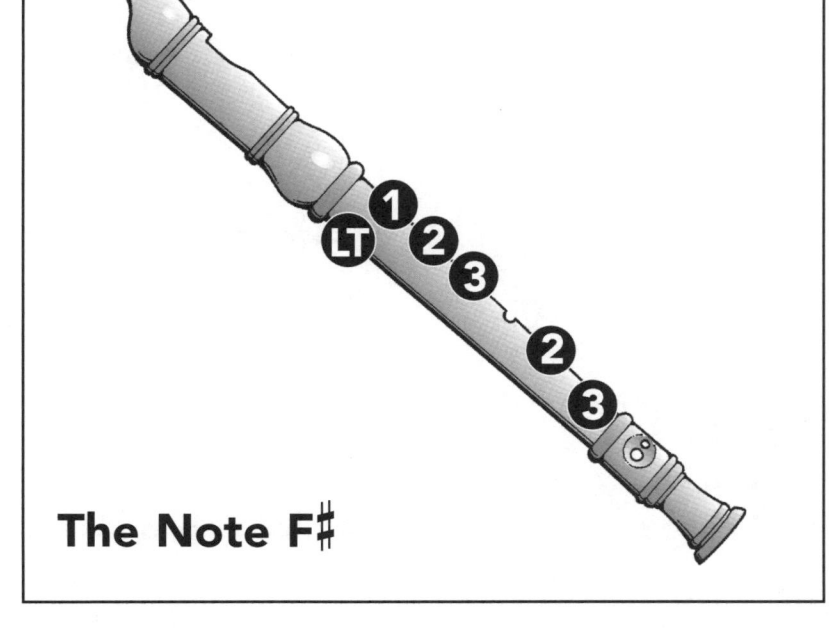

The Note F#

 **34**

 **35**

Here is another example which uses the **F#** note. Be sure to tongue all the eighth notes as there are no slurs in this tune.

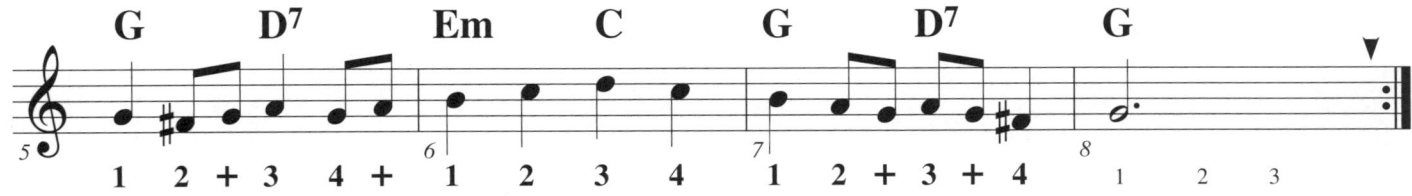

KEY SIGNATURES

Instead of writing a sharp sign before every **F#** note, it is easier to write just one sharp sign after the treble clef. This means that **all** F notes on the staff are played as **F#**, even though there is no sharp sign placed before the note. This is called a **Key Signature**. For more information on key signatures, see *Progressive Beginner Recorder Supplement*.

 36   The Galway Piper

Play all F notes as **F#** as indicated by the key signature.

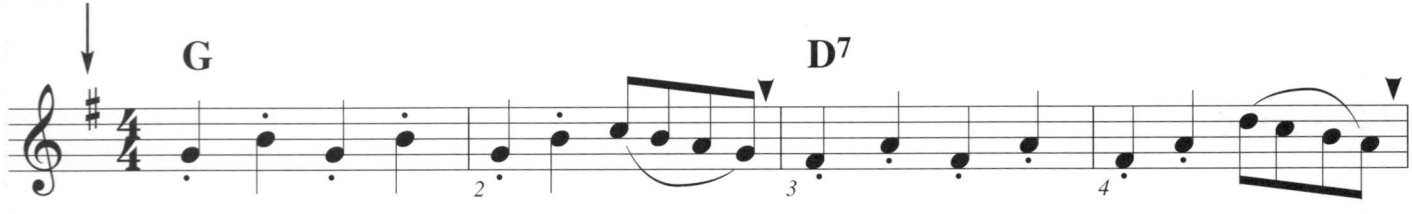

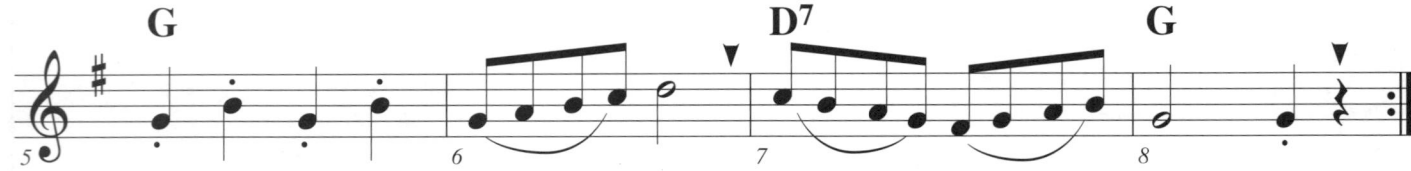

THE TIE

A **tie** is a curved line which connects two notes with the **same** position on the staff. The tie tells you to tongue the **first** note only, and to hold it for the length of both notes.

 **37**   Play the G note and hold it for six beats.

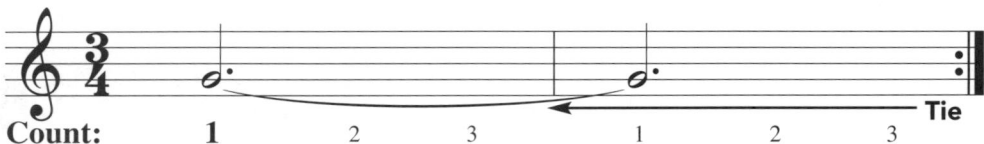

 **38   Mary Ann**

This Carribbean folk song contains ties and also uses a key signature.

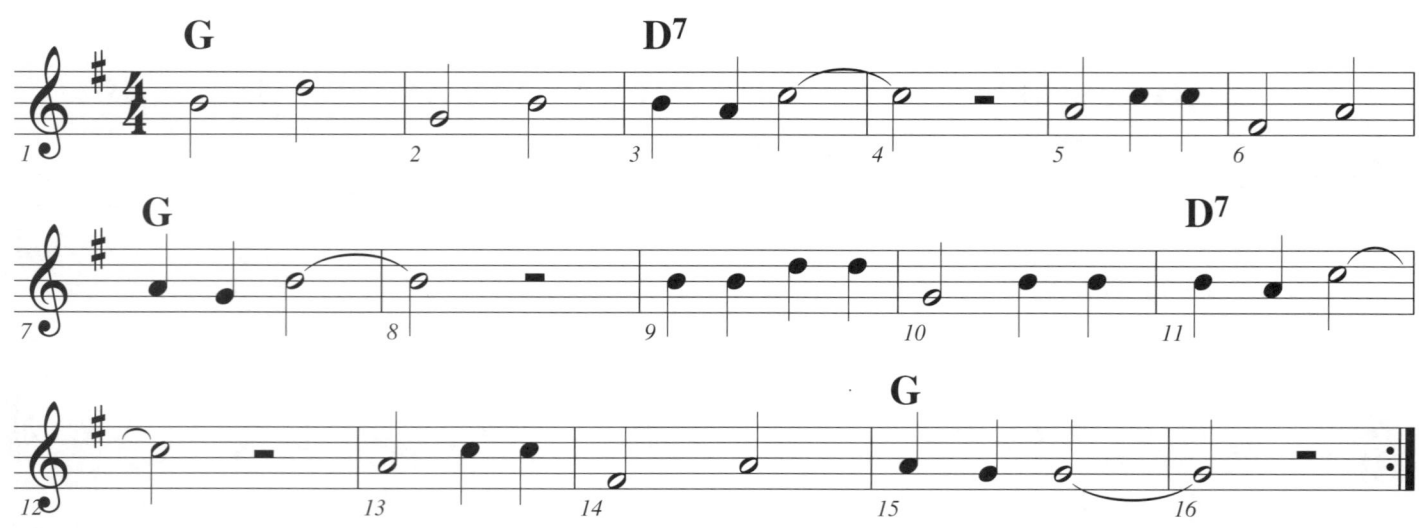

LESSON NINE

THE NOTE E

E Note

The note **E** is written on the **first** line of the staff.

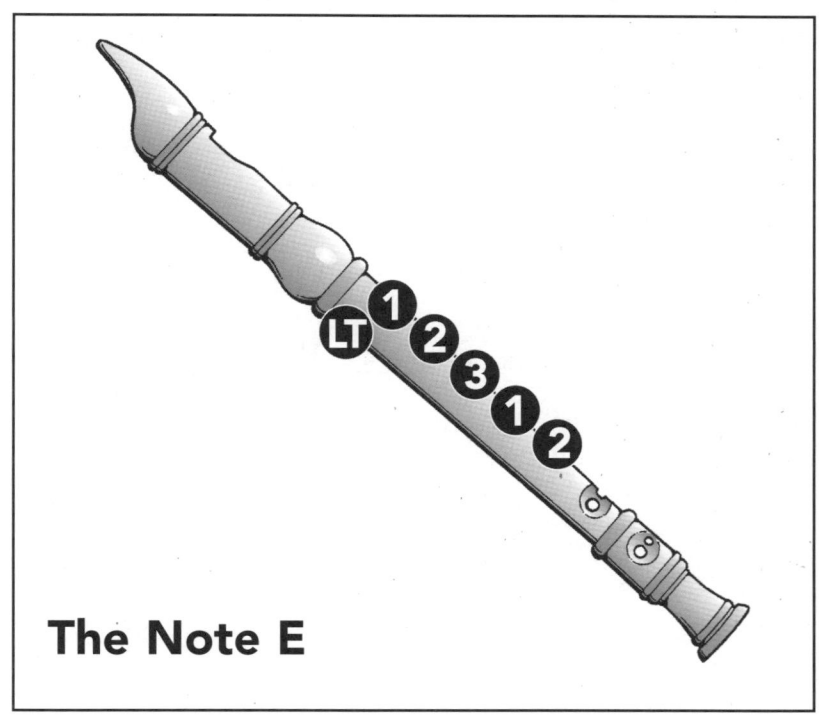

The Note E

 **39**

This example alternates between the notes **E** and **F♯**. Take care with the timing of the tied notes in the last bar.

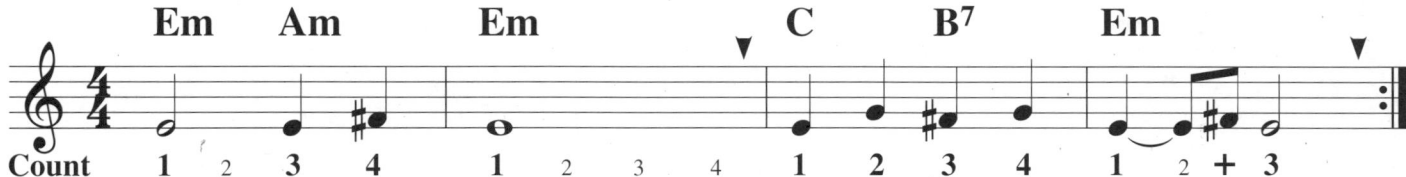

 **40** **The Volga Boatman**

Here is a traditional Russian song which features the note **E**. Notice also the key signature reminding you to play all F notes as **F♯**

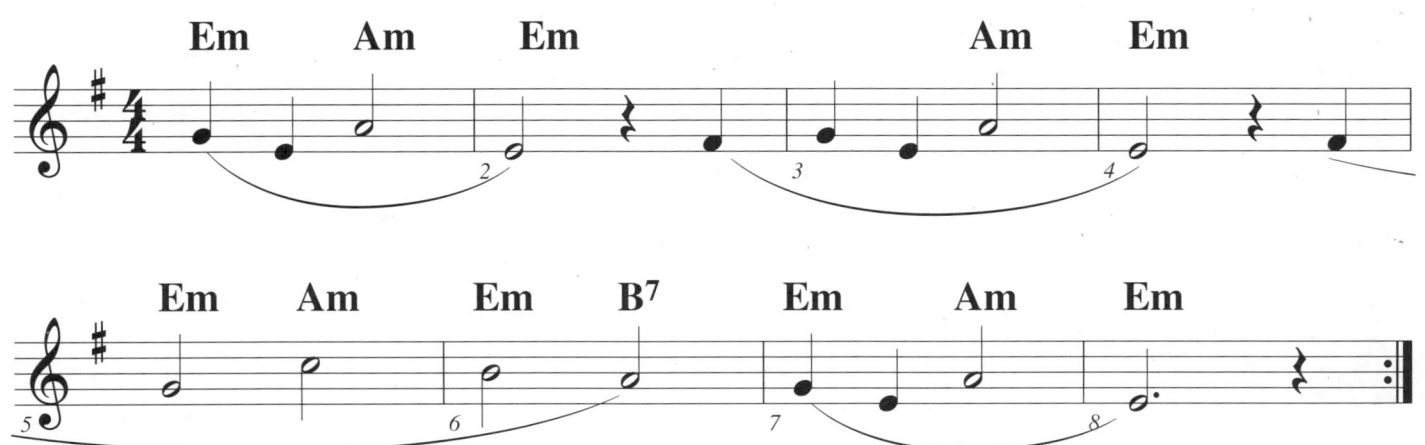

THE COMMON TIME SIGNATURE

 This symbol is called **common time**. It means exactly the same as 4/4 time.

The following examples are written in Common time and make use of the note **E** along with most of the other notes you have learnt. Take each one slowly at first and remember to play with a strong, even tone.

 **41   Gyspy Dance**

 **42**

This example is slightly more difficult. It makes frequent use of the note **E** and also features slurs covering groups of notes.

LESSON TEN

THE NOTE LOW D

D Note

This note **D** is written in the space **below** the staff.

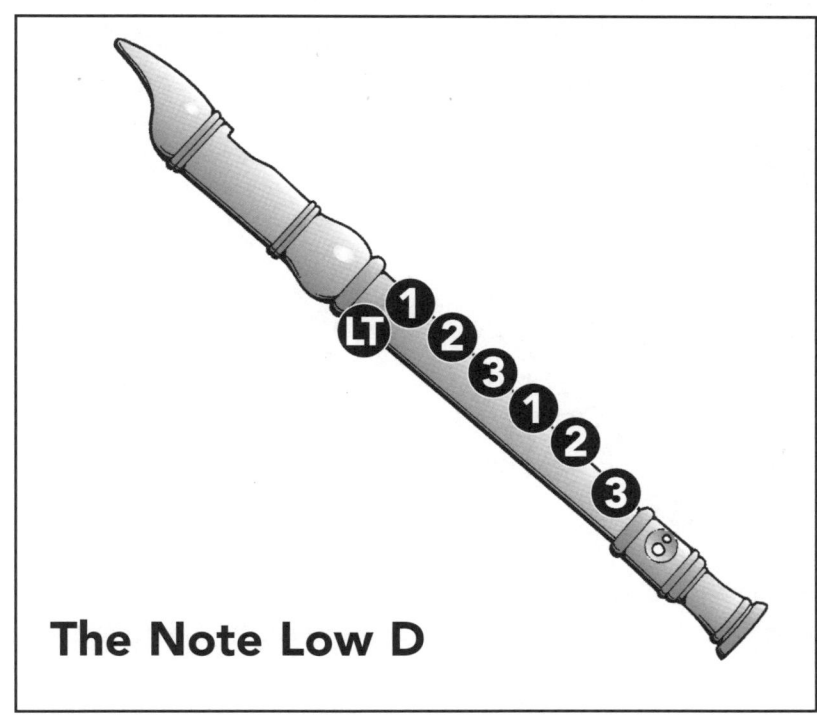

The Note Low D

 **43**

This example makes repeated use of the low **D** note. As with all new notes, memorize the fingering well and play tunes containing the new note slowly at first.

 **44**

THE OCTAVE

You have now learnt notes using all the different letter names used in music - **A**, **B**, **C**, **D**, **E**, **F** and **G**. Although there are only seven different letter names for notes, these notes are repeated on higher and lower pitches. The distance between a note and its repeat after passing all of the other letter names is called an **octave**. This term comes from the latin word for eight. If you start on the note low **D** and count up to the next **D** note, you will find that it is eight notes above the low **D**. Practice alternating between the low and high **D** notes as shown in the following example.

45

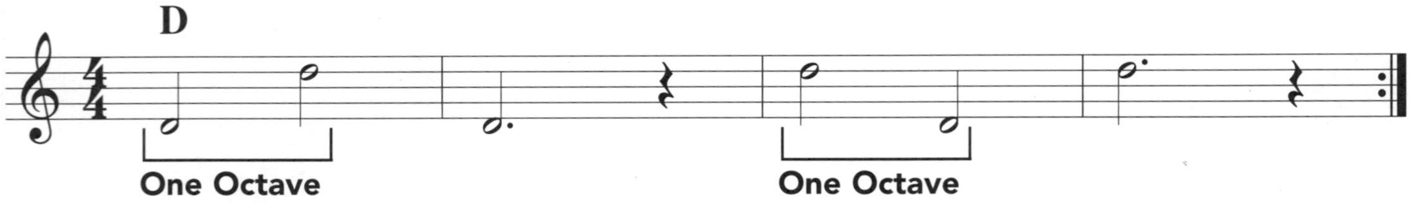

46

This example alternates between low **D** and all the other notes you have learnt before arriving at the **D** note one octave higher. The order is then reversed on the way back down.

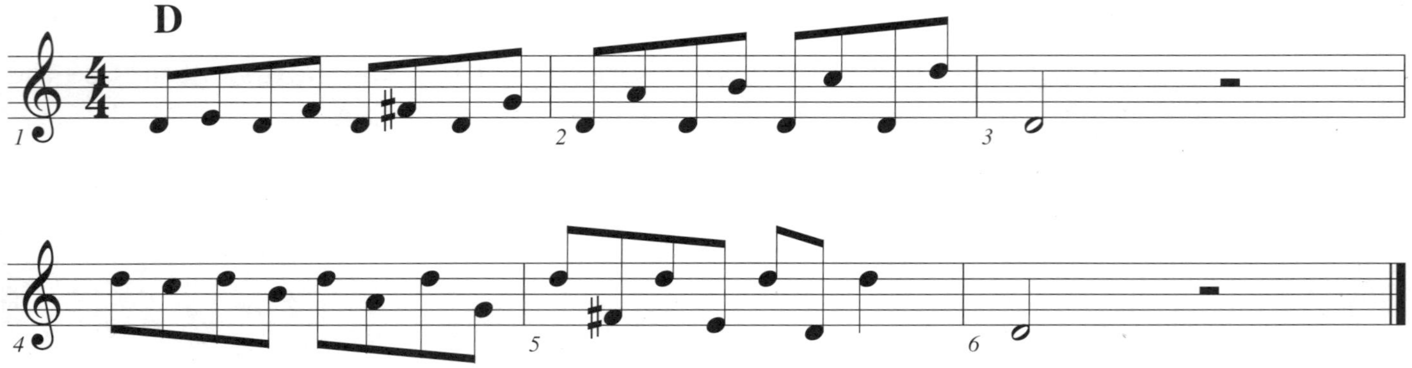

47 We Wish You a Merry Christmas

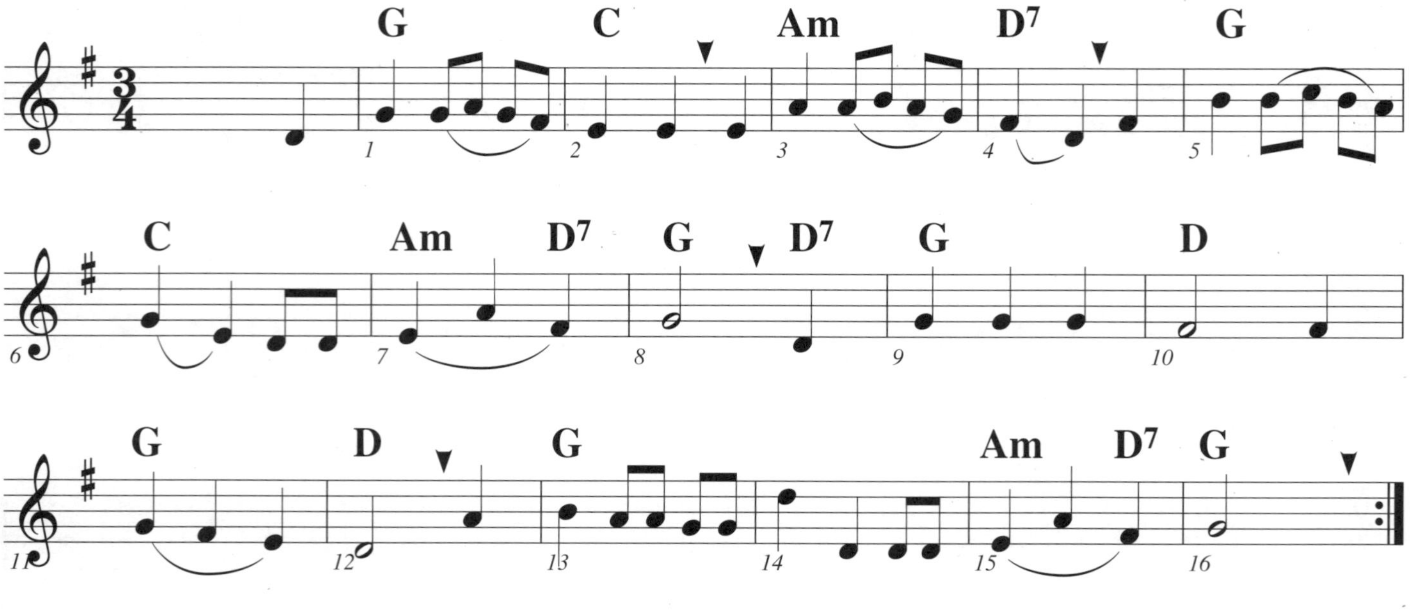

48 Shortnin' Bread

Here is another version of the children's song you learnt in lesson seven. Although the melody is the same, the actual notes are different because it is written here in the key of **D** instead of **F**, which means the melody is based around the note **D** and the previous version was based around the note **F**. It is possible to start any melody on any of the notes used in music. Because of the fingerings and techniques used on different musical instruments, the same key can be easy to play in on one instrument and difficult on another. For this reason it is common to change the key of a piece of music. Changing music from one key to another is called transposing. For more information on transposing, see *Progressive Beginner Recorder Supplement*.

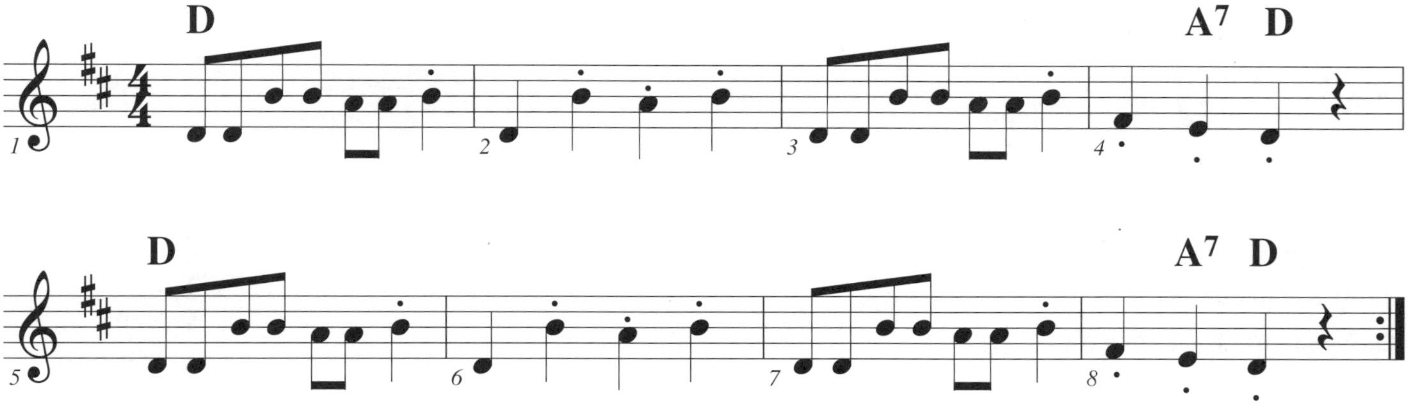

49 Goodnight Irene

LESSON ELEVEN

THE NOTE LOW C

C Note

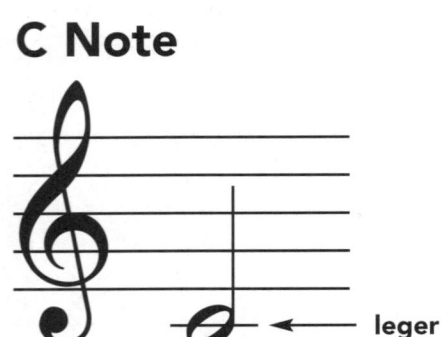

← leger line

Low C is written just below the staff on a short line called a **leger line.** This is the lowest note that can be played on the recorder.

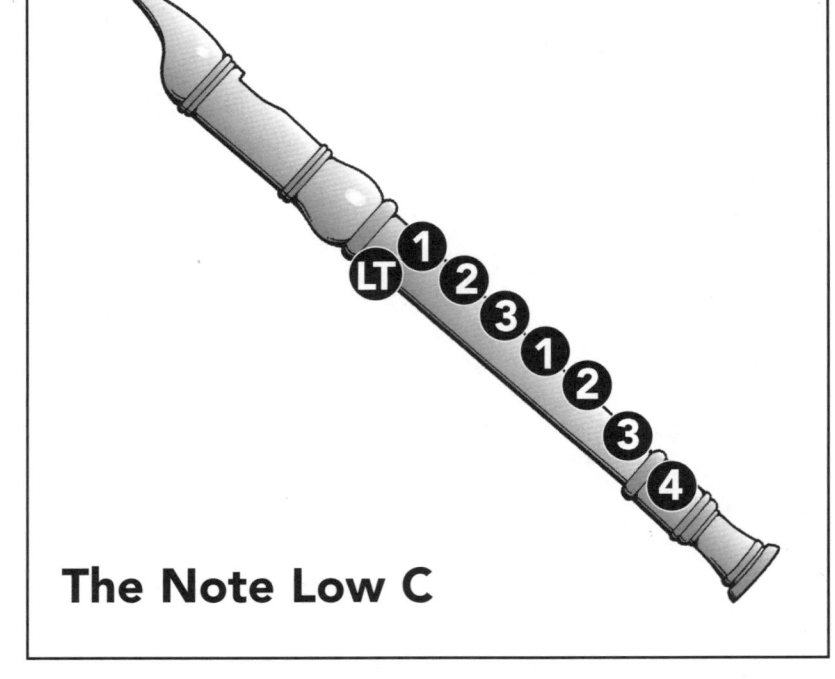

The Note Low C

 50

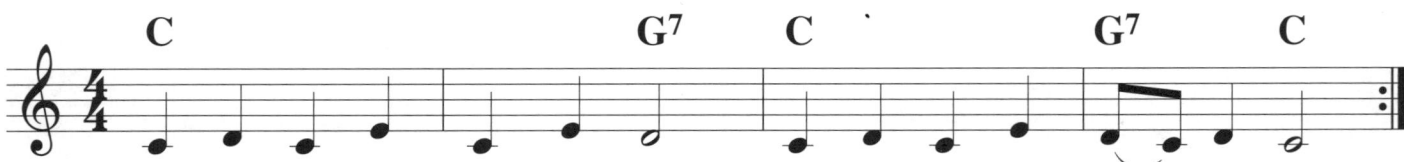

THE C MAJOR SCALE

A **major scale** is a group of eight notes that produces the familiar sound:

        Do Re Mi Fa So La Ti Do

You now know enough notes to play the **C major scale**.

        C D E F G A B C

 51

The number underneath each note indicates its position in the scale. These numbers are called **scale degrees**. As with the two **D** notes you have learnt, the distance between the low **C** and the higher **C** at the top of the major scale is one octave.

MARCH

INDIAN CHANT

American

15. JUBA

American Folk S

Ju - ba this and Ju - ba that, Ju - ba saw a yel - low cat.

Ju - ba up and Ju - ba down, Ju - ba run - ning all a - round.

This land is your land, This land is my land,

From Cal - i - for - nia to the New York is - land,

From the red-wood for - est to the Gulf Stream wa - ters;

This land was made for you and me.

THE KEY OF C MAJOR

When a song consists of notes from a particular scale, it is said to be written in the **key** which has the same name as that scale. For example, if a song contains notes from the **C major scale**, it is said to be in the **key of C major**. The following song is written in the key of C major.

52 Lavender's Blue

The following examples will help to build your playing technique and consolidate your knowledge of the notes you have learnt. They are all based around the C major scale. Take them slowly at first and be sure to sound each note clearly and evenly.

53

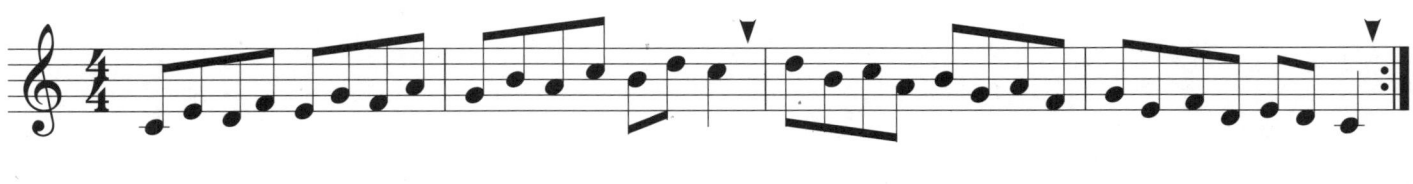

54

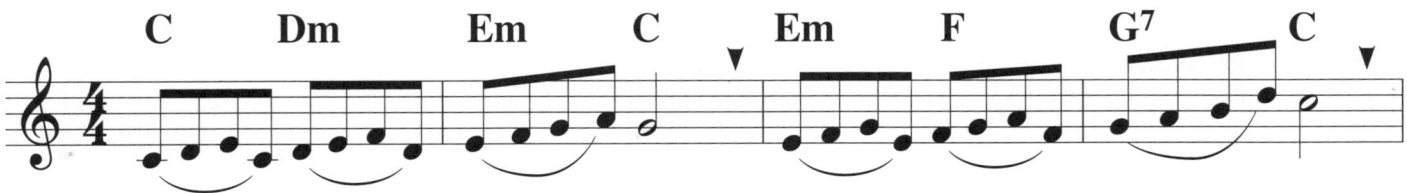

55

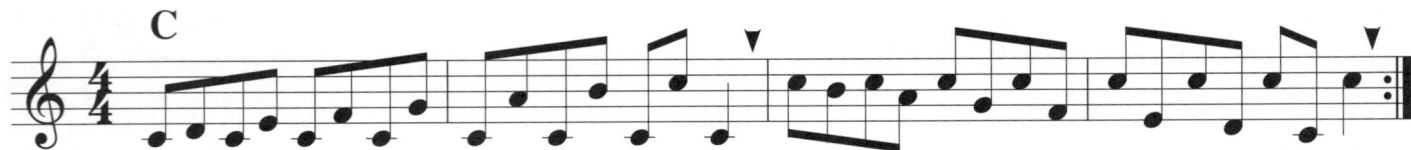

56 Botany Bay

This traditional Australian song is also derived from the C major scale. There are literally hundreds of songs which can be played using only the notes of the C major scale.

LESSON TWELVE

THE DOTTED QUARTER NOTE

A dot written after a quarter note means that you hold the note for **one and a half beats**.

Count 1 2 +

A dotted quarter note is often followed by an eighth note.

57

58

Here is another example to help you become familiar with dotted quarter notes.

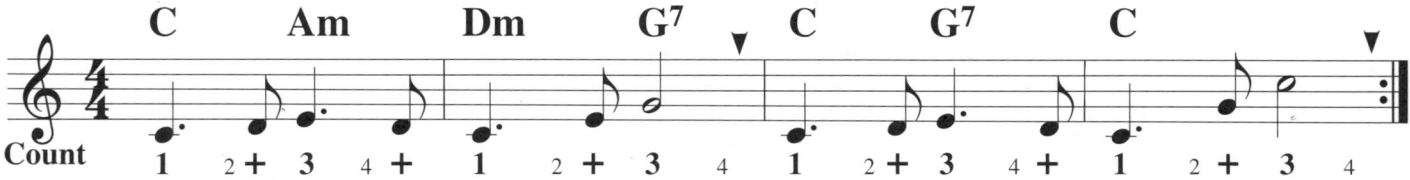

59 Morning Has Broken

FIRST AND SECOND ENDINGS

The following song contains **first and second endings**. The **first** time you play through the song, play the **first ending** (|1.   ⌐), then go back to the beginning. The **second** time you play through the song, play the **second ending** (|2.   ⌐) instead of the first. Notice also the use of dotted quarter notes in bars 3 and 5.

60   Jingle Bells

61   Mussi Den

Here is another song which uses first and second endings. In this one, the second ending leads into a whole new section.

SYNCOPATION

 **62**

Here is another rhythm figure using dotted quarter notes. This time the eighth note is played first and the dotted quarter note is played off the beat. This creates an effect known as **syncopation**, which means displacing the normal flow of accents, usually from **on** the beat to **off** the beat. Practice this example slowly at first and count carefully as you play.

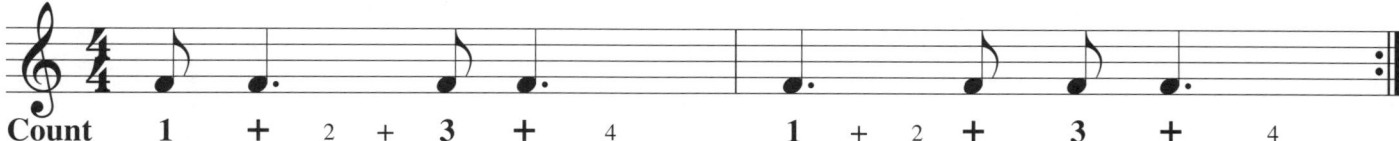

 **63   Swing Low, Sweet Chariot**

This well known spiritual makes frequent use of the syncopated rhythm shown above. If you have trouble with any of the timing in this song, practice the rhythm figures on one note at first as in the previous example.

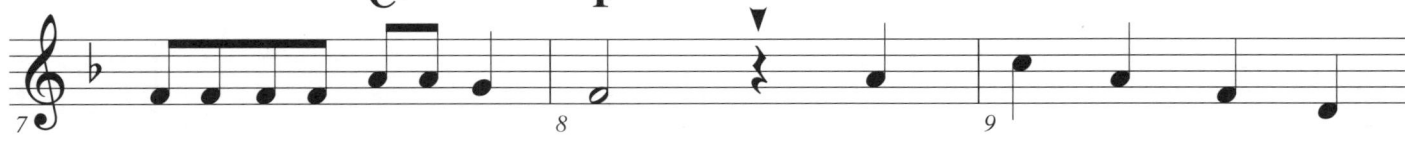
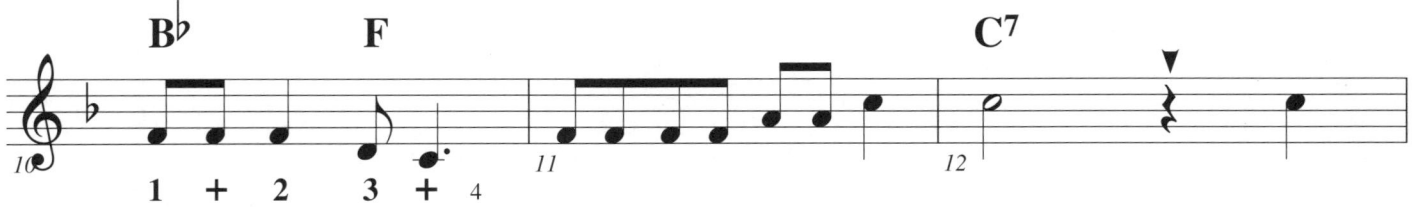

Here are two more songs which contain syncopated rhythms. Take each one slowly at first and remember to count mentally as you play. Tapping your foot on each beat is another useful method of helping to keep good time when playing syncopated rhythms.

 **64   Tom Dooley**

 **65   The Sloop John B**

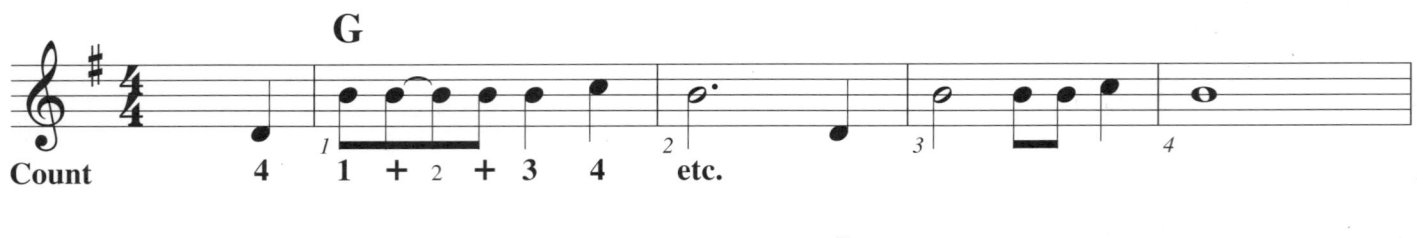

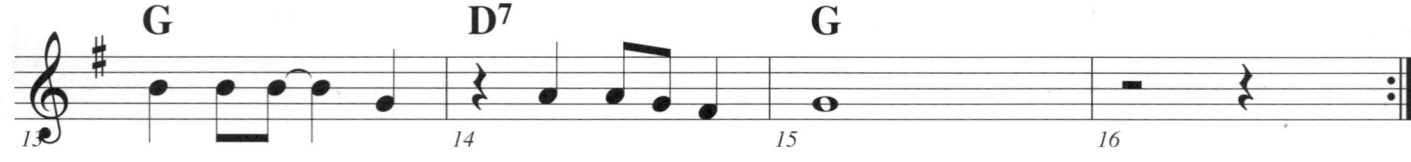

LESSON THIRTEEN

FLAT SIGNS

♭ This is a **flat** sign.

When a flat sign is placed in front of a note, it **lowers** the pitch of the note by an interval known as one **semitone** or one **half step**. Thus the note **B♭** is one semitone **lower** than B. Since the difference in pitch between the notes A and B is one **whole tone** (two semitones or one **whole step**), **B♭** is also one semitone **higher** than **A**.

THE NOTE B♭

B♭ (B Flat) Note

A flat sign is always placed **before** the note.

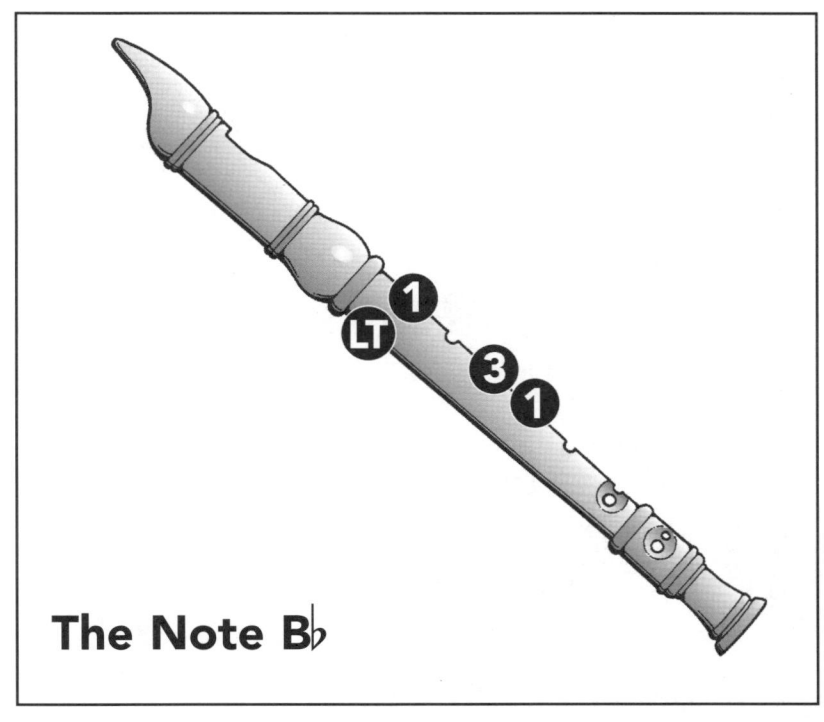

The Note B♭

 **66**

Like the sharp sign, the flat sign affects **all** B notes within the bar in which it appears. Eg: in bars 1, 3 and 5 the ♭ sign appears before the first B in each bar. The flat also applies to all other B notes within that particular bar. The effect of a flat sign is **cancelled by a bar line**, meaning that a **new** flat sign is needed to indicate a new **B♭** note in the following bar.

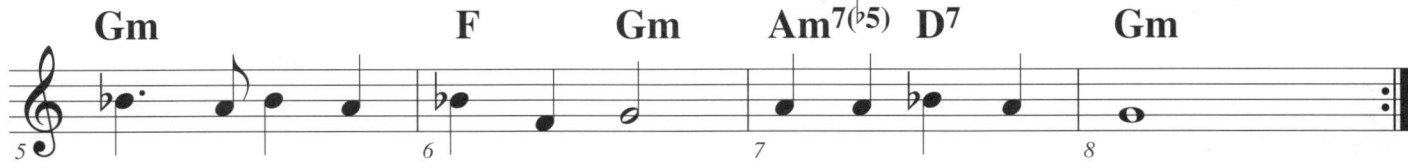

FLAT KEY SIGNATURES

Just as when you are dealing with sharps, it is possible to use a key signature to indicate that all B notes are to be played as B♭ as shown in the following songs.

 **67 All Through the Night**

Play all B notes as B♭ as indicated by the key signature.

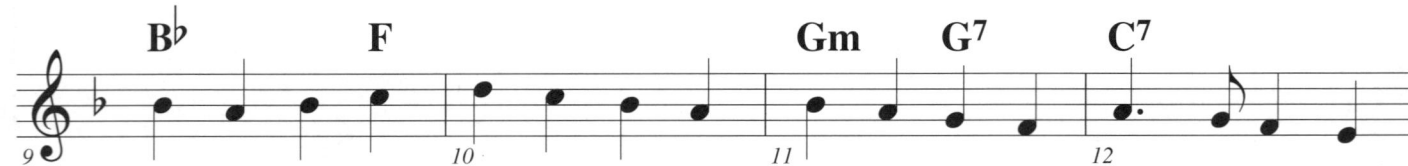
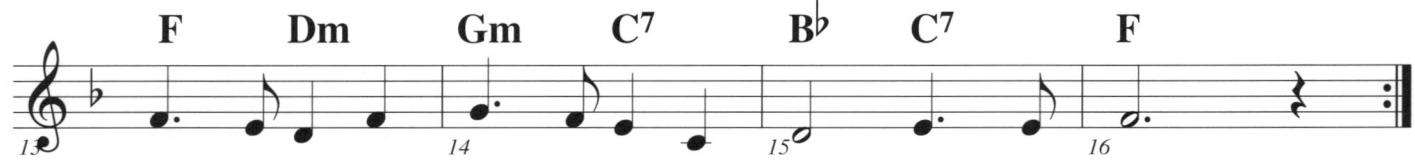

 **68 Oh Susanna**

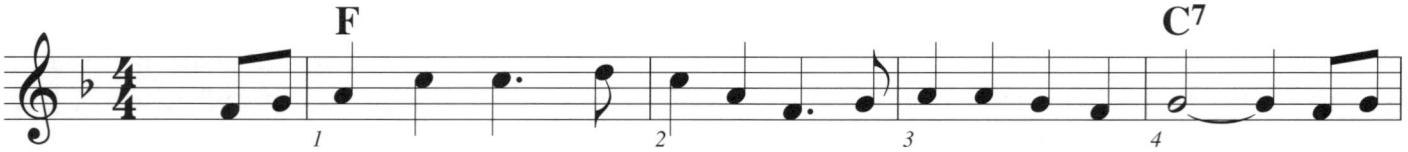

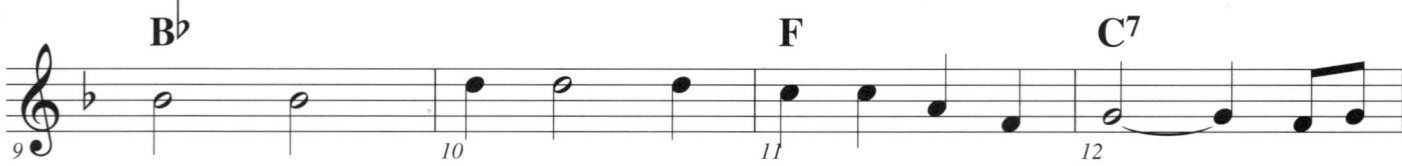

The next two songs are written in a different type of key called a **minor key**. Minor keys are often described as having a sadder sound than major keys. For more information on minor keys, see *Progressive Beginner Recorder Supplement*.

 **69 God Rest Ye Merry Gentlemen**

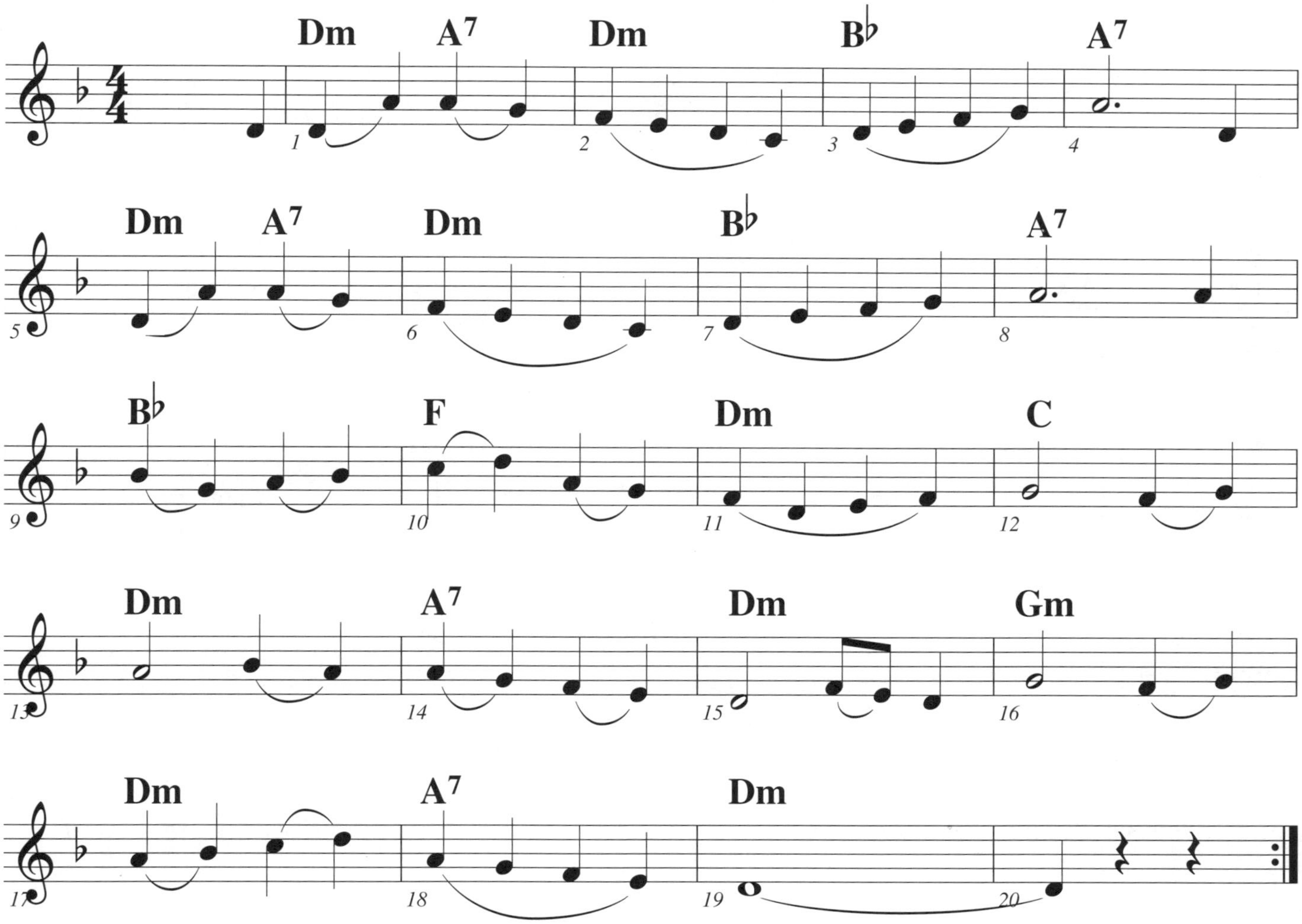

70 In Olden Days

LESSON FOURTEEN

THE NOTE HIGH E

E Note

This note **E** is written in the **fourth** space of the staff.

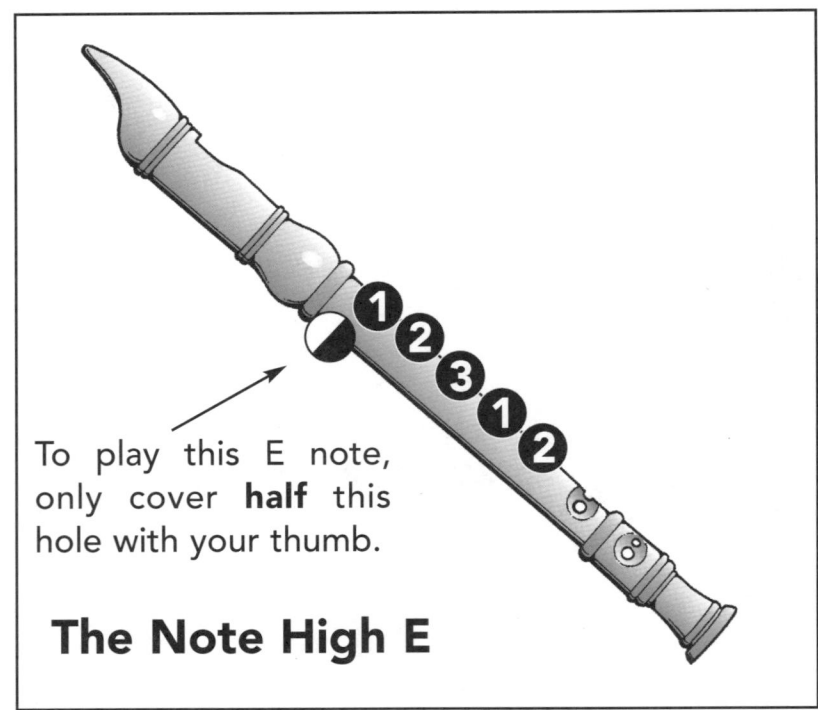

To play this E note, only cover **half** this hole with your thumb.

The Note High E

 **71**

A good way to begin playing the high **E** note is to practice changing octaves between this note and the low **E** note. The only fingering change required is the movement of the left thumb between completely covering the hole (low E) and half covering the hole (high E).

 **72**

Changing between high **E** and other notes may be difficult at first. Play the following example slowly and deliberately until you can confidently change between all the notes. Make sure each note sounds clearly and evenly.

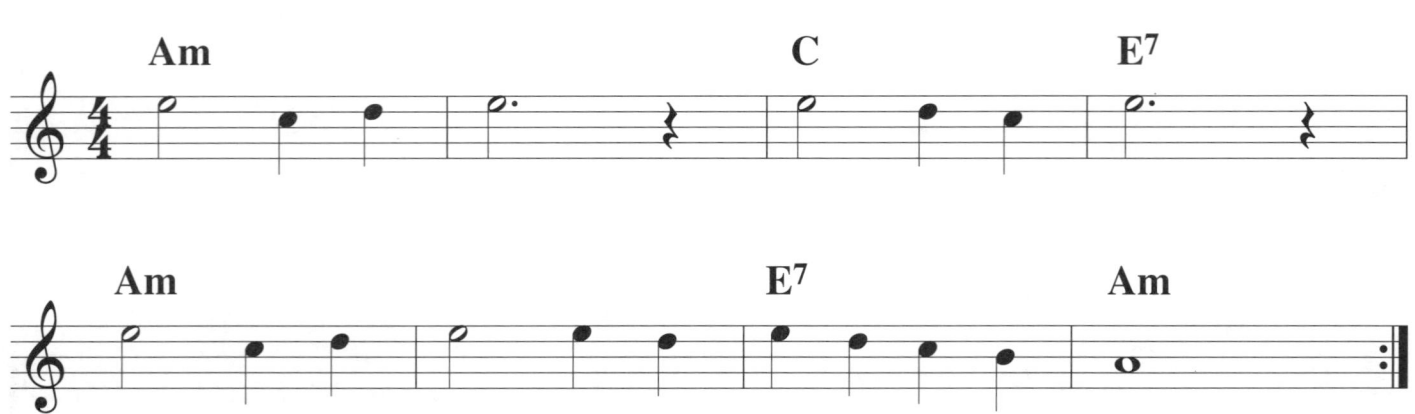

Here are some more examples which make use of the high **E** note.

 **73**

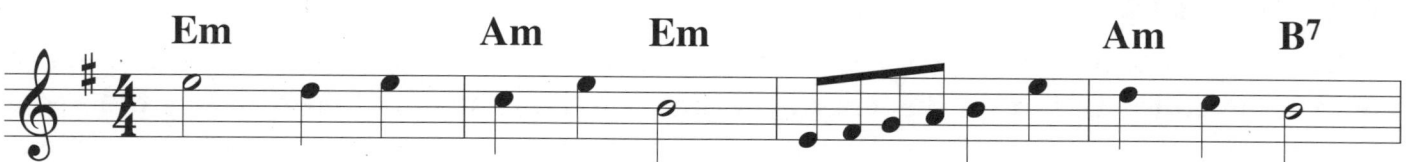

 **74 My Bonnie Lies Over the Ocean**

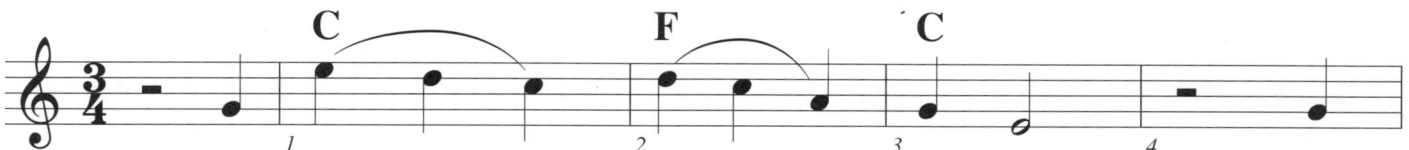

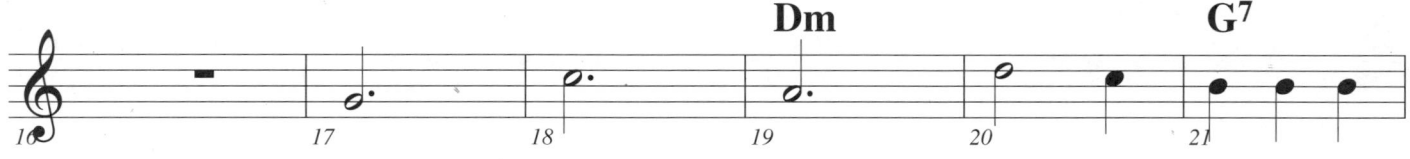
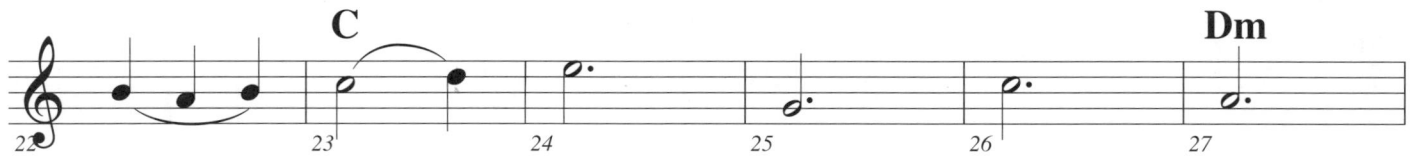
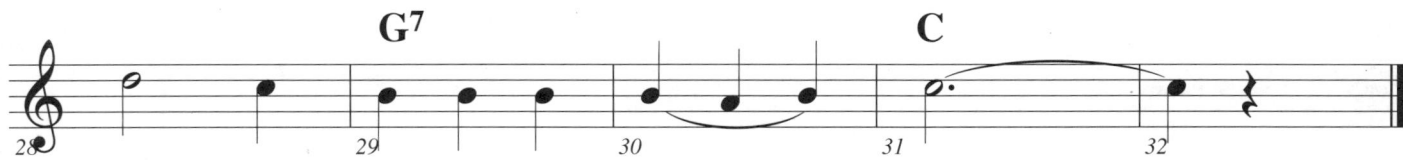

LESSON FIFTEEN

12 BAR BLUES

12 Bar Blues is a pattern of chords which repeats every 12 bars. There are hundreds of well known songs based on this chord progression, i.e., they contain basically the same chords in the same order. 12 bar Blues is one of the most common progressions in Blues, Jazz and Rock. 12 bar Blues songs are very common in modern saxophone, clarinet and trumpet music. Since many people learn the recorder as a first step towards learning these instruments, it is important to become familiar with this musical form. Every recorder player will be regularly asked to play a 12 bar Blues. In fact it is very likely to be the first progression used at any jam session.

Some well known Rock 'N' Roll songs which use this 12 bar chord pattern are:

Original Batman T.V. Theme
Hound Dog - Elvis Presley
Rock Around The Clock - Bill Haley
Roll Over Beethoven - Chuck Berry
Blue Suede Shoes - Elvis Presley
In The Mood - Glen Miller

Shake, Rattle and Roll - Bill Haley
Barbara Ann - The Beach Boys
Johnny B. Goode - Chuck Berry
Dizzy Miss Lizzy - The Beatles
Surfin' U.S.A. - The Beach Boys
Good Golly Miss Molly - Little Richard

RIFFS

One very common musical technique in Jazz, Blues and Rock playing is the use of riffs. A **riff** is a short musical idea (usually one or two bars long) which is repeated throughout a song. A riff can be altered and varied (e.g. played at different pitches) to fit a chord progression. Here is an example of a riff applied to the 12 bar Blues progression.

 75

THE EIGHTH REST

 This is an **eighth rest**.
It indicates **half a beat of silence**.

76

The use of eighth rests on the beat is a very common way of achieving syncopated rhythms.

The following example demonstrates a common way of using eighth rests. Remember to count in your mind to keep time while you are playing.

77

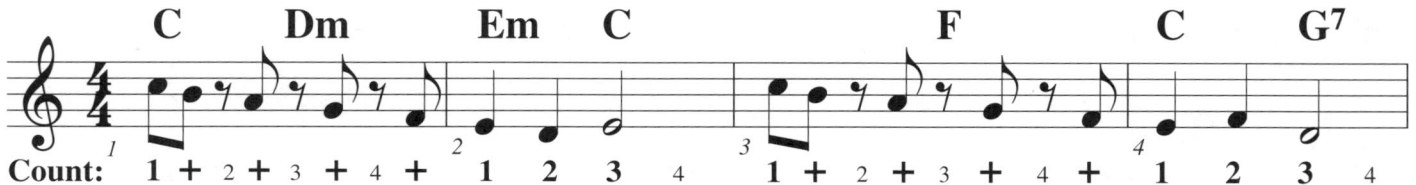

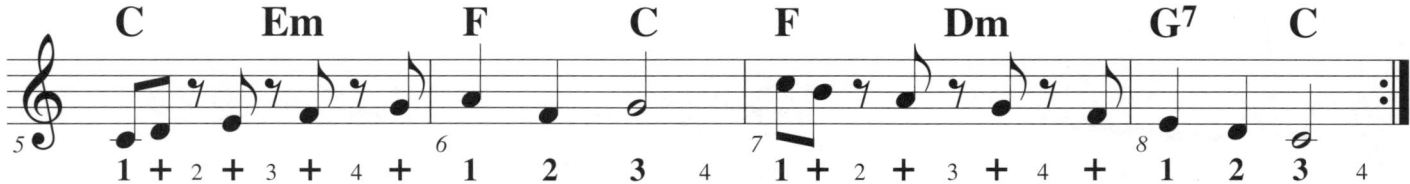

THE NATURAL SIGN

 This is a **natural** sign.

A natural sign cancels the effect of a sharp or flat for the rest of that bar, or until another sharp or flat sign occurs within that bar. Notice the alternation between F natural and F sharp in example 78.

78

One of the most common uses of the natural sign is to temporarily cancel the effect of a key signature. In the following example, the key signature indicates that F notes are to be played as F♯, so a natural sign is needed to indicate the F♮ in each bar.

79

80 Creepy Blues

This 12 bar Blues makes use of sharp, flat and natural signs.

LESSON SIXTEEN

THE TRIPLET

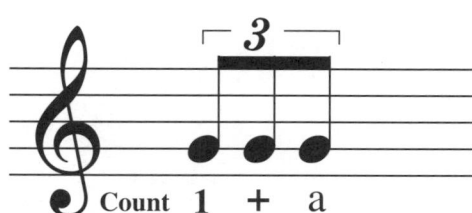

A **triplet** is a group of **three** evenly spaced notes played within one beat. Eighth note triplets are indicated by three eighth notes grouped together by a bracket (or a curved line) and the numeral **3**. The eighth note triplets are played with one third of a beat each. Triplets are easy to understand once you have heard them played. Listen to example 81 on the CD to hear the effect of triplets.

 **81   How to Count Triplets**

The following 12 bar Blues demonstrates the use of triplets. As with any new rhythm you learn, count as you play and tap your foot on the beat to help you keep time.

 **82   Triplet Blues**

SWING RHYTHMS

A **swing rhythm** can be created by tying together the first and second notes of a triplet. There are several different ways of writing swing rhythms. To understand them it is worth using one musical example written in various ways. First play example 83 which contains eighth note triplets.

Example 84 has the first and second notes of the triplet group tied. This gives the example a swing feel.

The two eighth note triplets tied together in example 84 can be replaced by a quarter note.

To simplify notation, it is common to replace the ♪♪ with ♩♪, and to write at the start of the piece ♪♪ = ♩♪ as illustrated below in example 86.

Examples 84, 85, and 86 sound **exactly the same** but are just written differently.

Here are some examples which contain swing rhythms. Remember, although the eighth notes are written as normal, they are played as swing eighths as indicated by the symbol before the start of each example.

87 Riffin' the Blues

88 St James Infirmary

This traditional New Orleans song has been played by many of the Jazz greats and was made famous by **Louis Armstrong**.

 ## 89   Battle Hymn of the Republic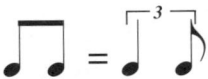

Notice that there are no slurs in this song. This means you will need to tongue all of the notes, even when there are many consecutive eighth notes.

Here is a final example which contains both swing, eighth notes and triplets. For more songs to play as well as valuable additional information on major and minor keys, transposing, extra notes and extra rhythms, it is recommended that you move on to *Progressive Beginner Recorder Supplement* on completion of this book.

 ## 90   Swing That Thing

INDEX OF FINGERINGS

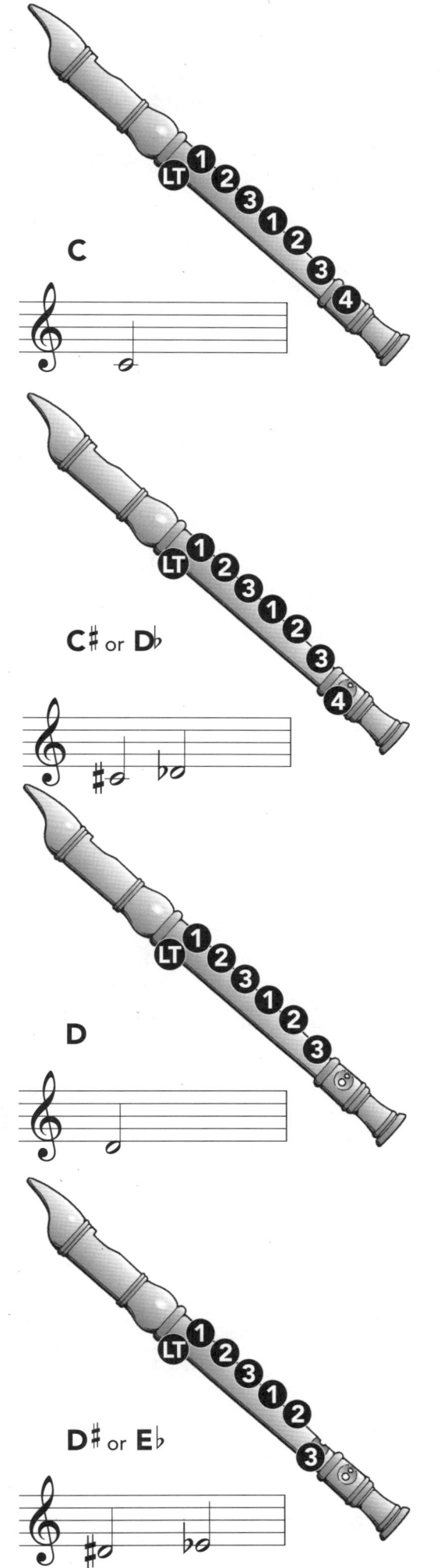

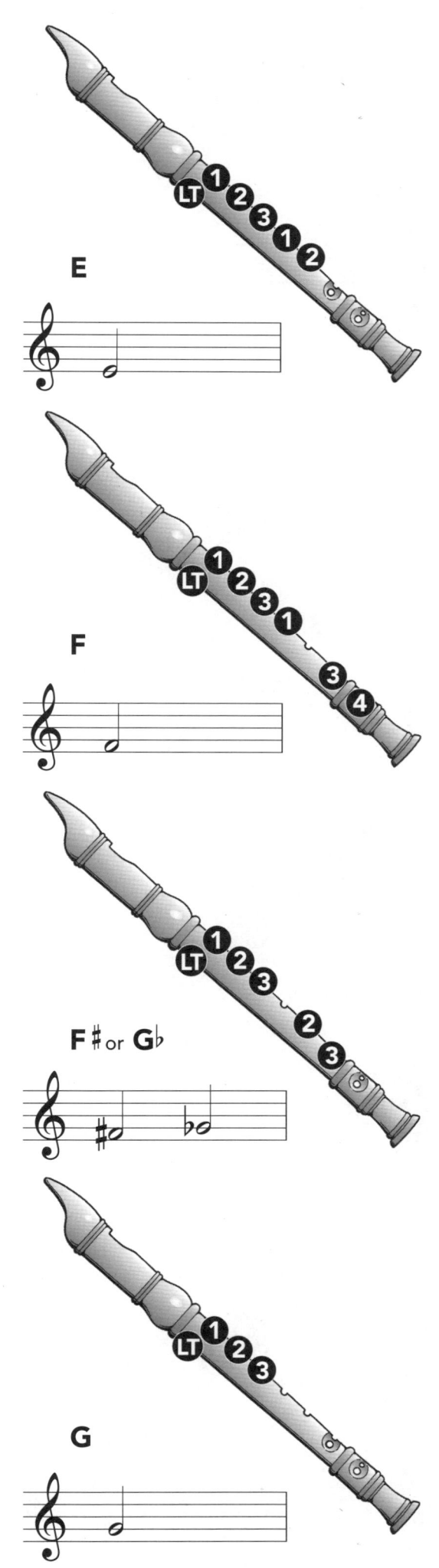

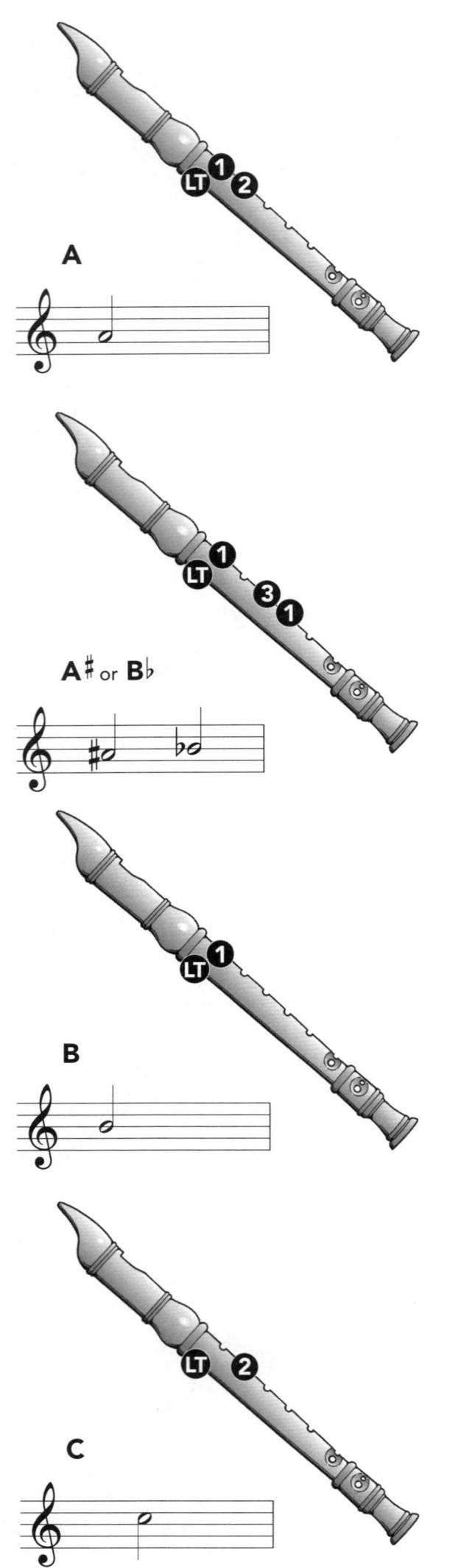
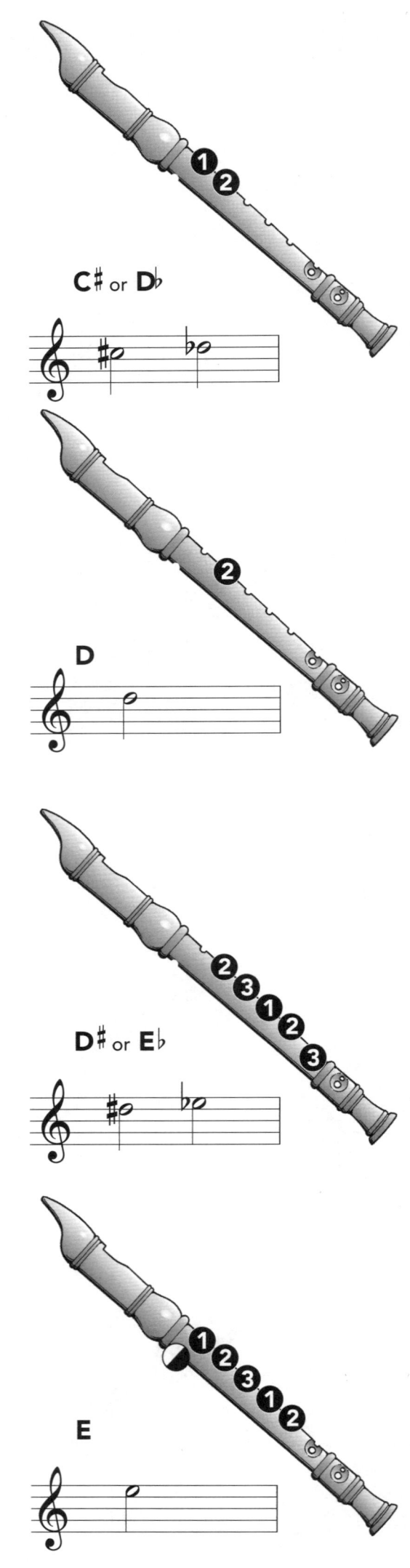

GLOSSARY OF MUSICAL TERMS

Accidental — a sign used to show a temporary change in pitch of a note (i.e. sharp ♯, flat ♭, double sharp ✘, double flat ♭♭, or natural ♮). The sharps or flats in a key signature are not regarded as accidentals.

Ad lib — to be played at the performer's own discretion.

Allegretto — moderately fast.

Allegro — fast and lively.

Andante — an easy walking pace.

Arpeggio — the playing of a chord in single note fashion.

Bar — a division of music occurring between two bar lines (also called a 'measure').

Bar line — a vertical line drawn across the staff dividing the music into equal sections called bars.

Bass — the lower regions of pitch in general. On guitar, the 4th, 5th and 6th strings.

Chord — a combination of three or more different notes played together.

Chord progression — a series of chords played as a musical unit (e.g. as in a song).

Clef — a sign placed at the beginning of each staff of music which fixes the location of a particular note on the staff, and hence the location of all other notes.

Coda — an ending section of music, signified by the sign ⊕.

Common time — and indication of $\frac{4}{4}$ time — four quarter note beats per bar (also indicated by 𝄴).

D.C al fine — a repeat from the sign (indicated thus 𝄋) to the word 'fine'.

Dynamics — the varying degrees of softness (indicated by the term 'piano') and loudness (indicated by the term 'forte') in music.

Eighth note — a note with the value of half a beat in $\frac{4}{4}$ time, indicated thus ♪ (also called a quaver).

The eighth note rest — indicating half a beat of silence is written: 𝄾

Enharmonic — describes the difference in notation, but not in pitch, of two notes.

Fermata — a sign, ⌢, used to indicate that a note or chord is held to the player's own discretion (also called a 'pause sign').

Flat — a sign, (♭) used to lower the pitch of a note by one semitone.

Forte — loud. Indicated by the sign f.

Half note — a note with the value of two beats in 4/4 time, indicated thus: 𝅗𝅥 (also called a minim). The half note rest, indicating two beats of silence, is written: ▬ on the third staff line.

Harmony — the simultaneous sounding of two or more different notes.

Interval — the distance between any two notes of different pitches.

Key — describes the notes used in a composition in regards to the major or minor scale from which they are taken; e.g. a piece 'in the key of C major' describes the melody, chords, etc., as predominantly consisting of the notes, **C, D, E, F, G, A,** and **B** — i.e. from the **C** scale.

Key signature — a sign, placed at the beginning of each stave of music, directly after the clef, to indicate the key of a piece. The sign consists of a certain number of sharps or flats, which represent the sharps or flats found in the scale of the piece's key.

Leger lines — small horizontal lines upon which notes are written when their pitch is either above or below the range of the staff.

Legato — smoothly, well connected.

Lick — a short musical phrase.

Major scale — a series of eight notes in alphabetical order based on the interval sequence tone - tone - semitone - tone - tone - tone - semitone, giving the familiar sound **do re mi fa so la ti do**.

Melody — a group of notes of varying pitch and duration, and having a recognizable musical shape.

Metronome — a device which indicates the number of beats per minute, and which can be adjusted in accordance to the desired tempo.

Moderato — at a moderate pace. **Natural** — a sign (♮) used to cancel out the effect of a sharp or flat. The word is also used to describe the notes **A, B, C, D, E, F** and **G**; e.g. 'the natural notes'.

Note — a single sound with a given pitch and duration.

Octave — the distance between any given note with a set frequency, and another note with exactly double that frequency. Both notes will have the same letter name.

Open voicing — a chord that has the notes spread out between both hands on the keyboard.

Pitch — the sound produced by a note, determined by the frequency of the string vibrations. The pitch relates to a note being referred to as 'high' or 'low'.

Plectrum — a small object (often of a triangular shape) made of plastic which is used to pick or strum the strings of a guitar.

Quarter note — a note with the value of one beat in 4/4 time, indicated thus ♩ (also called a crotchet).

The quarter note rest, indicating one beat of silence, is written: 𝄽 .

Repeat signs — used to indicate a repeat of a section of music, by means of two dots placed before a double bar line.

Rhythm — the note after which a chord or scale is named (also called 'key note').

Riff — a repeating pattern which may be altered to fit chord changes.

Semitone — the smallest interval used in conventional music. On guitar, it is a distance of one fret.

Sharp — a sign (♯) used to raise the pitch of a note by one semitone.

Staccato — to play short and detached. Indicated by a dot placed above the note.

Staff — five parallel lines together with four spaces, upon which music is written.

Syncopation — the placing of an accent on a normally unaccented beat.

Tempo — the speed of a piece.

Tie — a curved line joining two or more notes of the same pitch, where the second note(s) is not played, but its time value is added to that of the first note.

Timbre — a quality which distinguishes a note produced on one instrument from the same note produced on any other instrument (also called 'tone colour'). A given note on the guitar will sound different (and therefore distinguishable) from the same pitched note on piano, violin, flute etc. There is usually also a difference in timbre from one guitar to another.

Time signature — a sign at the beginning of a piece which indicates, by means of figures, the number of beats per bar (top figure), and the type of note receiving one beat (bottom figure).

Tone — a distance of two frets; i.e. the equivalent of two semitones.

Transposition — the process of changing music from one key to another.

Treble — the upper regions of pitch in general.

Treble clef — a sign placed at the beginning of the staff to fix the pitch of the notes placed on it. The treble clef (also called 'G clef') is placed so that the second line indicates as G note.

PROGRESSIVE ROCK SAXOPHONE METHOD

FOR BEGINNER TO ADVANCED STUDENTS

Specifically designed for students wishing to play Rock sax, either in a group or solo for fun. The emphasis is on making music immediately. Covers a variety of sounds, rhythms and techniques essential to Rock playing. Also contains lessons on transposing, playing in all keys and improvisation. Anyone who completes this book will be well on the way to becoming an excellent Rock sax player

PROGRESSIVE BEGINNER SAXOPHONE

FOR BEGINNING SAXOPHONISTS

A great introduction to the fundamentals of Saxophone playing and understanding music. All examples sound great and are fun to play. Covers a variety of styles including Rock, Jazz, Blues, Pop and Classical, along with an introduction to improvising.

PROGRESSIVE BEGINNER FLUTE

FOR BEGINNING FLUTE PLAYERS

A great introduction to the fundamentals of Flute playing and understanding music. All examples sound great and are fun to play. Covers a variety of styles including Classical, Jazz, Blues, Pop and Rock, along with an introduction to improvising.

PROGRESSIVE BEGINNER CLARINET

FOR BEGINNING CLARINET PLAYERS

A great introduction to the fundamentals of Clarinet playing and understanding music. All examples sound great and are fun to play. Covers a variety of styles including Classical, Jazz, Blues, Pop and Rock, along with an introduction to improvising.

PROGRESSIVE BEGINNER TRUMPET

FOR BEGINNING TRUMPET PLAYERS

A great introduction to the fundamentals of Trumpet playing and understanding music. All examples sound great and are fun to play. Covers a variety of styles including Rock, Jazz, Pop, Classical, and Blues, along with an introduction to improvising.